68 Pizza Recipes for Home

By: Kelly Johnson

Table of Contents

- Margherita Pizza
- Pepperoni Pizza
- Veggie Supreme Pizza
- BBQ Chicken Pizza
- Hawaiian Pizza
- Meat Lover's Pizza
- Buffalo Chicken Pizza
- White Pizza with Ricotta and Spinach
- Mediterranean Pizza
- Pesto Chicken Pizza
- Mushroom and Truffle Oil Pizza
- Caprese Pizza
- Taco Pizza
- Sausage and Onion Pizza
- Greek Pizza
- Shrimp Scampi Pizza
- Breakfast Pizza
- Fig and Prosciutto Pizza
- Philly Cheesesteak Pizza
- Chicken Alfredo Pizza
- Artichoke and Olive Pizza
- Spinach and Feta Pizza
- Roasted Red Pepper and Goat Cheese Pizza
- BLT Pizza
- Caramelized Onion and Gorgonzola Pizza
- Thai Chicken Pizza
- Clam and Garlic Pizza
- Sun-Dried TOmato and Basil Pizza
- Buffalo Cauliflower Pizza
- S'mores Dessert Pizza
- Caramel Apple Dessert Pizza
- Chicken Pesto Flatbread
- Margherita Naan Pizza
- Roasted Veggie Naan Pizza
- Prosciutto and Arugula Flatbread
- Fig and Goat Cheese Flatbread

- Ratatouille Pizza
- Mediterranean Flatbread
- BBQ Pulled Pork Pizza
- Bruschetta Pizza
- Pear and Gorgonzola Pizza
- Buffalo Ranch Chicken Pizza
- Asparagus and Parmesan Pizza
- Quattro Formaggi Pizza
- Philly Cheesesteak Flatbread
- CHicken Tikka Masala Pizza
- Reuben Pizza
- Caramelized Pear and Brie Pizza
- Buffalo Cauliflower Flatbread
- SMoked Salmon and Cream Cheese Pizza
- Sweet Potato and Kale Pizza
- Provolone and Mushroom Pizza
- Artichoke and Sun-Dried Tomato Flatbread
- Smoky BBQ Bacon Pizza
- Roasted Garlic and Potato Pizza
- Bacon, Egg and Cheese Breakfast Pizza
- Chicken and Broccoli Alfredo Pizza
- Tandoori Chicken Naan Pizza
- Caramelized Onion and Bacon Flatbread
- Mediterranean Chicken Pita Pizza
- Apple, Bacon and Cheddar Pizza
- Buffalo Cauliflower and Blue Cheese Flatbread
- Shrimp and Avocado Flatbread
- Spinach and Artichoke Dip Pizza
- Pear and Walnut Flatbread
- Turkey and Cranberry Pizza
- Fig and Prosciutto Flatbread
- Smoked Gouda and Caramelized Onion Pizza

Margherita Pizza

Ingredients:

Pizza Dough:

- 2 1/4 teaspoons (1 packet) active dry yeast
- 1 teaspoon sugar
- 3/4 cup warm water (110°F/43°C)
- 2 cups all-purpose flour
- 1 teaspoon salt
- 1 tablespoon olive oil

Pizza Toppings:

- 1 cup tomato sauce (homemade or store-bought)
- 8 ounces fresh mozzarella, sliced
- Fresh basil leaves
- 2 tablespoons olive oil
- Salt and pepper to taste

Instructions:

Prepare the Pizza Dough:
- In a small bowl, combine the warm water, sugar, and active dry yeast. Let it sit for about 5-10 minutes, or until it becomes frothy.
- In a large mixing bowl, combine the flour and salt. Make a well in the center and pour in the yeast mixture and olive oil.
- Mix until the dough comes together, then knead on a floured surface for about 5-7 minutes, or until the dough is smooth and elastic.
- Place the dough in a lightly oiled bowl, cover it with a damp cloth, and let it rise in a warm place for 1-2 hours or until it has doubled in size.

Preheat the Oven:
- Preheat your oven to the highest temperature it can go (usually around 475-500°F/245-260°C). If you have a pizza stone, place it in the oven during preheating.

Shape the Pizza Dough:

- Punch down the risen dough and transfer it to a floured surface. Roll it out into your desired pizza shape and thickness.

Assemble the Pizza:
- If using a pizza stone, transfer the rolled-out dough onto a pizza peel dusted with flour or cornmeal. If not using a stone, place the rolled-out dough on a lightly greased baking sheet.
- Spread an even layer of tomato sauce over the dough, leaving a small border around the edges.
- Arrange the slices of fresh mozzarella on top of the sauce.
- Drizzle the pizza with olive oil and season with salt and pepper to taste.

Bake the Pizza:
- If using a pizza stone, carefully transfer the pizza onto the preheated stone in the oven. If not using a stone, simply place the baking sheet in the oven.
- Bake for about 10-12 minutes or until the crust is golden and the cheese is bubbly and slightly browned.

Finish and Serve:
- Remove the pizza from the oven, sprinkle fresh basil leaves over the top, and let it cool for a few minutes before slicing.
- Serve hot and enjoy your delicious Margherita Pizza!

Feel free to adjust the quantities and ingredients according to your preferences.

Pepperoni Pizza

Ingredients:

Pizza Dough:

- 2 1/4 teaspoons (1 packet) active dry yeast
- 1 teaspoon sugar
- 3/4 cup warm water (110°F/43°C)
- 2 cups all-purpose flour
- 1 teaspoon salt
- 1 tablespoon olive oil

Pizza Toppings:

- 1 cup pizza sauce (homemade or store-bought)
- 2 cups shredded mozzarella cheese
- 1/2 cup sliced pepperoni
- 1/4 cup grated Parmesan cheese
- 1 teaspoon dried oregano
- Red pepper flakes (optional)
- Olive oil for brushing

Instructions:

Prepare the Pizza Dough:
- In a small bowl, combine the warm water, sugar, and active dry yeast. Let it sit for about 5-10 minutes, or until it becomes frothy.
- In a large mixing bowl, combine the flour and salt. Make a well in the center and pour in the yeast mixture and olive oil.
- Mix until the dough comes together, then knead on a floured surface for about 5-7 minutes, or until the dough is smooth and elastic.
- Place the dough in a lightly oiled bowl, cover it with a damp cloth, and let it rise in a warm place for 1-2 hours or until it has doubled in size.

Preheat the Oven:
- Preheat your oven to the highest temperature it can go (usually around 475-500°F/245-260°C). If you have a pizza stone, place it in the oven during preheating.

Shape the Pizza Dough:

- Punch down the risen dough and transfer it to a floured surface. Roll it out into your desired pizza shape and thickness.

Assemble the Pizza:
- If using a pizza stone, transfer the rolled-out dough onto a pizza peel dusted with flour or cornmeal. If not using a stone, place the rolled-out dough on a lightly greased baking sheet.
- Spread an even layer of pizza sauce over the dough, leaving a small border around the edges.
- Sprinkle the shredded mozzarella cheese evenly over the sauce.
- Arrange the pepperoni slices on top of the cheese.
- Sprinkle grated Parmesan cheese and dried oregano over the pizza. Add red pepper flakes if you like a bit of heat.
- Optionally, brush the crust with olive oil for a golden finish.

Bake the Pizza:
- If using a pizza stone, carefully transfer the pizza onto the preheated stone in the oven. If not using a stone, simply place the baking sheet in the oven.
- Bake for about 10-12 minutes or until the crust is golden, the cheese is melted and bubbly, and the pepperoni is slightly crispy.

Finish and Serve:
- Remove the pizza from the oven, let it cool for a few minutes, and then slice it into wedges.
- Serve hot and enjoy your delicious Pepperoni Pizza!

Feel free to customize the toppings and crust thickness to suit your preferences.

Veggie Supreme Pizza

Ingredients:

Pizza Dough:

- 2 1/4 teaspoons (1 packet) active dry yeast
- 1 teaspoon sugar
- 3/4 cup warm water (110°F/43°C)
- 2 cups all-purpose flour
- 1 teaspoon salt
- 1 tablespoon olive oil

Pizza Toppings:

- 1 cup pizza sauce (homemade or store-bought)
- 2 cups shredded mozzarella cheese
- 1/2 cup sliced bell peppers (assorted colors)
- 1/2 cup sliced red onions
- 1/2 cup sliced black olives
- 1/2 cup sliced mushrooms
- 1/2 cup cherry tomatoes, halved
- 1/4 cup artichoke hearts, drained and sliced
- 1/4 cup crumbled feta cheese
- 1 teaspoon dried oregano
- Olive oil for brushing

Instructions:

Prepare the Pizza Dough:
- In a small bowl, combine the warm water, sugar, and active dry yeast. Let it sit for about 5-10 minutes, or until it becomes frothy.
- In a large mixing bowl, combine the flour and salt. Make a well in the center and pour in the yeast mixture and olive oil.
- Mix until the dough comes together, then knead on a floured surface for about 5-7 minutes, or until the dough is smooth and elastic.
- Place the dough in a lightly oiled bowl, cover it with a damp cloth, and let it rise in a warm place for 1-2 hours or until it has doubled in size.

Preheat the Oven:

- Preheat your oven to the highest temperature it can go (usually around 475-500°F/245-260°C). If you have a pizza stone, place it in the oven during preheating.

Shape the Pizza Dough:
- Punch down the risen dough and transfer it to a floured surface. Roll it out into your desired pizza shape and thickness.

Assemble the Pizza:
- If using a pizza stone, transfer the rolled-out dough onto a pizza peel dusted with flour or cornmeal. If not using a stone, place the rolled-out dough on a lightly greased baking sheet.
- Spread an even layer of pizza sauce over the dough, leaving a small border around the edges.
- Sprinkle the shredded mozzarella cheese evenly over the sauce.
- Arrange the sliced bell peppers, red onions, black olives, mushrooms, cherry tomatoes, and artichoke hearts on top of the cheese.
- Sprinkle crumbled feta cheese and dried oregano over the pizza.
- Optionally, brush the crust with olive oil for a golden finish.

Bake the Pizza:
- If using a pizza stone, carefully transfer the pizza onto the preheated stone in the oven. If not using a stone, simply place the baking sheet in the oven.
- Bake for about 10-12 minutes or until the crust is golden, the cheese is melted and bubbly, and the veggies are tender.

Finish and Serve:
- Remove the pizza from the oven, let it cool for a few minutes, and then slice it into wedges.
- Serve hot and enjoy your delicious Veggie Supreme Pizza!

Feel free to customize the vegetable toppings based on your preferences.

BBQ Chicken Pizza

Ingredients:

Pizza Dough:

- 2 1/4 teaspoons (1 packet) active dry yeast
- 1 teaspoon sugar
- 3/4 cup warm water (110°F/43°C)
- 2 cups all-purpose flour
- 1 teaspoon salt
- 1 tablespoon olive oil

Pizza Toppings:

- 1/2 cup barbecue sauce (store-bought or homemade)
- 2 cups cooked and shredded chicken (rotisserie chicken works well)
- 1 1/2 cups shredded mozzarella cheese
- 1/2 cup red onion, thinly sliced
- 1/4 cup fresh cilantro, chopped
- 1/4 cup corn kernels (optional)
- 1/4 cup crumbled feta cheese (optional)
- Olive oil for brushing

Instructions:

Prepare the Pizza Dough:
- In a small bowl, combine the warm water, sugar, and active dry yeast. Let it sit for about 5-10 minutes, or until it becomes frothy.
- In a large mixing bowl, combine the flour and salt. Make a well in the center and pour in the yeast mixture and olive oil.
- Mix until the dough comes together, then knead on a floured surface for about 5-7 minutes, or until the dough is smooth and elastic.
- Place the dough in a lightly oiled bowl, cover it with a damp cloth, and let it rise in a warm place for 1-2 hours or until it has doubled in size.

Preheat the Oven:
- Preheat your oven to the highest temperature it can go (usually around 475-500°F/245-260°C). If you have a pizza stone, place it in the oven during preheating.

Shape the Pizza Dough:

- Punch down the risen dough and transfer it to a floured surface. Roll it out into your desired pizza shape and thickness.

Assemble the Pizza:
- If using a pizza stone, transfer the rolled-out dough onto a pizza peel dusted with flour or cornmeal. If not using a stone, place the rolled-out dough on a lightly greased baking sheet.
- Spread an even layer of barbecue sauce over the dough, leaving a small border around the edges.
- Sprinkle the shredded mozzarella cheese evenly over the sauce.
- Evenly distribute the shredded chicken and sliced red onions on top of the cheese.
- Optionally, add corn kernels and crumbled feta cheese for extra flavor.
- Optionally, brush the crust with olive oil for a golden finish.

Bake the Pizza:
- If using a pizza stone, carefully transfer the pizza onto the preheated stone in the oven. If not using a stone, simply place the baking sheet in the oven.
- Bake for about 10-12 minutes or until the crust is golden, the cheese is melted and bubbly, and the edges are slightly crispy.

Finish and Serve:
- Remove the pizza from the oven, sprinkle fresh cilantro over the top, and let it cool for a few minutes before slicing.
- Serve hot and enjoy your delicious BBQ Chicken Pizza!

Feel free to adjust the barbecue sauce quantity and add your favorite toppings to suit your taste.

Hawaiian Pizza

Ingredients:

Pizza Dough:

- 2 1/4 teaspoons (1 packet) active dry yeast
- 1 teaspoon sugar
- 3/4 cup warm water (110°F/43°C)
- 2 cups all-purpose flour
- 1 teaspoon salt
- 1 tablespoon olive oil

Pizza Toppings:

- 1 cup pizza sauce (homemade or store-bought)
- 2 cups shredded mozzarella cheese
- 1 cup cooked ham, diced
- 1 cup pineapple chunks (fresh or canned, drained)
- 1/4 cup red onion, thinly sliced
- 1/4 cup grated Parmesan cheese
- Olive oil for brushing (optional)

Instructions:

Prepare the Pizza Dough:
- In a small bowl, combine warm water, sugar, and active dry yeast. Let it sit for 5-10 minutes until frothy.
- In a large mixing bowl, combine the flour and salt. Make a well in the center and pour in the yeast mixture and olive oil.
- Mix until the dough comes together, then knead on a floured surface for 5-7 minutes or until smooth. Place the dough in an oiled bowl, cover with a damp cloth, and let it rise for 1-2 hours until doubled in size.

Preheat the Oven:
- Preheat your oven to the highest temperature it can go (typically around 475-500°F/245-260°C). If you have a pizza stone, place it in the oven during preheating.

Shape the Pizza Dough:

- Punch down the risen dough and transfer it to a floured surface. Roll it out into your desired pizza shape and thickness.

Assemble the Pizza:
- If using a pizza stone, transfer the rolled-out dough onto a pizza peel dusted with flour or cornmeal. If not using a stone, place the rolled-out dough on a lightly greased baking sheet.
- Spread an even layer of pizza sauce over the dough, leaving a small border around the edges.
- Sprinkle the shredded mozzarella cheese over the sauce.
- Distribute the diced ham, pineapple chunks, and thinly sliced red onion evenly over the pizza.
- Sprinkle grated Parmesan cheese over the top.
- Optionally, brush the crust with olive oil for a golden finish.

Bake the Pizza:
- If using a pizza stone, carefully transfer the pizza onto the preheated stone in the oven. If not using a stone, simply place the baking sheet in the oven.
- Bake for 10-12 minutes or until the crust is golden, the cheese is melted and bubbly, and the edges are slightly crispy.

Finish and Serve:
- Remove the pizza from the oven, let it cool for a few minutes, and then slice it into wedges.
- Serve hot and enjoy your delicious Hawaiian Pizza!

Feel free to adjust the toppings and quantities based on your preferences.

Meat Lover's Pizza

Ingredients:

Pizza Dough:

- 2 1/4 teaspoons (1 packet) active dry yeast
- 1 teaspoon sugar
- 3/4 cup warm water (110°F/43°C)
- 2 cups all-purpose flour
- 1 teaspoon salt
- 1 tablespoon olive oil

Pizza Toppings:

- 1 cup pizza sauce (homemade or store-bought)
- 2 cups shredded mozzarella cheese
- 1/2 cup cooked and crumbled sausage
- 1/2 cup pepperoni slices
- 1/2 cup sliced cooked bacon
- 1/2 cup sliced ham or Canadian bacon
- 1/4 cup sliced black olives
- 1/4 cup sliced red onion
- 1/4 cup grated Parmesan cheese
- 1 teaspoon dried oregano
- Olive oil for brushing

Instructions:

Prepare the Pizza Dough:
- In a small bowl, combine warm water, sugar, and active dry yeast. Let it sit for 5-10 minutes until frothy.
- In a large mixing bowl, combine the flour and salt. Make a well in the center and pour in the yeast mixture and olive oil.
- Mix until the dough comes together, then knead on a floured surface for 5-7 minutes or until smooth. Place the dough in an oiled bowl, cover with a damp cloth, and let it rise for 1-2 hours until doubled in size.

Preheat the Oven:

- Preheat your oven to the highest temperature it can go (typically around 475-500°F/245-260°C). If you have a pizza stone, place it in the oven during preheating.

Shape the Pizza Dough:
- Punch down the risen dough and transfer it to a floured surface. Roll it out into your desired pizza shape and thickness.

Assemble the Pizza:
- If using a pizza stone, transfer the rolled-out dough onto a pizza peel dusted with flour or cornmeal. If not using a stone, place the rolled-out dough on a lightly greased baking sheet.
- Spread an even layer of pizza sauce over the dough, leaving a small border around the edges.
- Sprinkle the shredded mozzarella cheese over the sauce.
- Evenly distribute the crumbled sausage, pepperoni slices, sliced bacon, sliced ham or Canadian bacon, black olives, and sliced red onion over the pizza.
- Sprinkle grated Parmesan cheese and dried oregano over the top.
- Optionally, brush the crust with olive oil for a golden finish.

Bake the Pizza:
- If using a pizza stone, carefully transfer the pizza onto the preheated stone in the oven. If not using a stone, simply place the baking sheet in the oven.
- Bake for 10-12 minutes or until the crust is golden, the cheese is melted and bubbly, and the edges are slightly crispy.

Finish and Serve:
- Remove the pizza from the oven, let it cool for a few minutes, and then slice it into wedges.
- Serve hot and enjoy your hearty Meat Lover's Pizza!

Feel free to customize the meat toppings based on your preferences.

Buffalo Chicken Pizza

Ingredients:

Pizza Dough:

- 2 1/4 teaspoons (1 packet) active dry yeast
- 1 teaspoon sugar
- 3/4 cup warm water (110°F/43°C)
- 2 cups all-purpose flour
- 1 teaspoon salt
- 1 tablespoon olive oil

Buffalo Chicken:

- 1 cup cooked and shredded chicken (rotisserie chicken works well)
- 1/4 cup buffalo sauce
- 2 tablespoons ranch or blue cheese dressing

Pizza Toppings:

- 1 cup shredded mozzarella cheese
- 1/4 cup crumbled blue cheese (optional)
- 1/4 cup sliced red onion
- 1/4 cup chopped celery
- 1 tablespoon chopped fresh cilantro or parsley (optional)
- Ranch or blue cheese dressing for drizzling
- Olive oil for brushing

Instructions:

Prepare the Pizza Dough:
- In a small bowl, combine warm water, sugar, and active dry yeast. Let it sit for 5-10 minutes until frothy.
- In a large mixing bowl, combine the flour and salt. Make a well in the center and pour in the yeast mixture and olive oil.
- Mix until the dough comes together, then knead on a floured surface for 5-7 minutes or until smooth. Place the dough in an oiled bowl, cover with a damp cloth, and let it rise for 1-2 hours until doubled in size.

Preheat the Oven:

- Preheat your oven to the highest temperature it can go (typically around 475-500°F/245-260°C). If you have a pizza stone, place it in the oven during preheating.

Shape the Pizza Dough:
- Punch down the risen dough and transfer it to a floured surface. Roll it out into your desired pizza shape and thickness.

Prepare the Buffalo Chicken:
- In a bowl, combine the shredded chicken with buffalo sauce and ranch or blue cheese dressing. Toss until the chicken is well coated.

Assemble the Pizza:
- If using a pizza stone, transfer the rolled-out dough onto a pizza peel dusted with flour or cornmeal. If not using a stone, place the rolled-out dough on a lightly greased baking sheet.
- Spread an even layer of shredded mozzarella cheese over the dough.
- Evenly distribute the buffalo chicken mixture, sliced red onion, and crumbled blue cheese (if using) on top of the cheese.
- Optionally, brush the crust with olive oil for a golden finish.

Bake the Pizza:
- If using a pizza stone, carefully transfer the pizza onto the preheated stone in the oven. If not using a stone, simply place the baking sheet in the oven.
- Bake for 10-12 minutes or until the crust is golden, the cheese is melted and bubbly, and the edges are slightly crispy.

Finish and Serve:
- Remove the pizza from the oven, drizzle with additional ranch or blue cheese dressing, sprinkle chopped celery and fresh cilantro or parsley over the top.
- Let it cool for a few minutes, then slice and serve your delicious Buffalo Chicken Pizza!

Feel free to adjust the buffalo sauce intensity and toppings based on your preferences.

White Pizza with Ricotta and Spinach

Ingredients:

Pizza Dough:

- 2 1/4 teaspoons (1 packet) active dry yeast
- 1 teaspoon sugar
- 3/4 cup warm water (110°F/43°C)
- 2 cups all-purpose flour
- 1 teaspoon salt
- 1 tablespoon olive oil

White Pizza Sauce:

- 2 tablespoons unsalted butter
- 2 tablespoons all-purpose flour
- 1 cup whole milk
- 1 cup shredded mozzarella cheese
- 1/2 cup grated Parmesan cheese
- 2 cloves garlic, minced
- Salt and pepper to taste
- 1/4 teaspoon dried oregano
- 1/4 teaspoon dried basil

Pizza Toppings:

- 1 cup fresh spinach leaves, washed and dried
- 1 cup ricotta cheese
- 1/4 cup grated Parmesan cheese
- Olive oil for brushing

Instructions:

Prepare the Pizza Dough:
- In a small bowl, combine warm water, sugar, and active dry yeast. Let it sit for 5-10 minutes until frothy.

- In a large mixing bowl, combine the flour and salt. Make a well in the center and pour in the yeast mixture and olive oil.
- Mix until the dough comes together, then knead on a floured surface for 5-7 minutes or until smooth. Place the dough in an oiled bowl, cover with a damp cloth, and let it rise for 1-2 hours until doubled in size.

Prepare the White Pizza Sauce:
- In a saucepan over medium heat, melt the butter. Add minced garlic and sauté for about 1 minute until fragrant.
- Whisk in the flour to create a roux. Cook for 1-2 minutes, stirring continuously.
- Gradually whisk in the milk, ensuring there are no lumps. Cook until the mixture thickens.
- Stir in the mozzarella and Parmesan cheeses until melted and smooth.
- Season with salt, pepper, dried oregano, and dried basil. Remove from heat.

Preheat the Oven:
- Preheat your oven to the highest temperature it can go (typically around 475-500°F/245-260°C). If you have a pizza stone, place it in the oven during preheating.

Shape the Pizza Dough:
- Punch down the risen dough and transfer it to a floured surface. Roll it out into your desired pizza shape and thickness.

Assemble the Pizza:
- If using a pizza stone, transfer the rolled-out dough onto a pizza peel dusted with flour or cornmeal. If not using a stone, place the rolled-out dough on a lightly greased baking sheet.
- Spread the white sauce evenly over the dough, leaving a small border around the edges.
- Distribute fresh spinach leaves over the sauce.
- Spoon dollops of ricotta cheese onto the pizza.
- Sprinkle grated Parmesan cheese over the top.
- Optionally, brush the crust with olive oil for a golden finish.

Bake the Pizza:
- If using a pizza stone, carefully transfer the pizza onto the preheated stone in the oven. If not using a stone, simply place the baking sheet in the oven.
- Bake for 10-12 minutes or until the crust is golden, the cheese is melted and bubbly, and the edges are slightly crispy.

Finish and Serve:

- Remove the pizza from the oven, let it cool for a few minutes, then slice and serve your delectable White Pizza with Ricotta and Spinach!

Feel free to add a drizzle of olive oil or a sprinkle of red pepper flakes for extra flavor, if desired.

Mediterranean Pizza

Ingredients:

Pizza Dough:

- 2 1/4 teaspoons (1 packet) active dry yeast
- 1 teaspoon sugar
- 3/4 cup warm water (110°F/43°C)
- 2 cups all-purpose flour
- 1 teaspoon salt
- 1 tablespoon olive oil

Mediterranean Toppings:

- 1/2 cup tomato sauce or pesto (homemade or store-bought)
- 1 1/2 cups shredded mozzarella cheese
- 1/2 cup cherry tomatoes, halved
- 1/4 cup Kalamata olives, sliced
- 1/4 cup artichoke hearts, drained and sliced
- 1/4 cup red onion, thinly sliced
- 1/4 cup crumbled feta cheese
- 1/4 cup fresh basil, chopped
- 1 tablespoon capers (optional)
- Olive oil for brushing

Instructions:

Prepare the Pizza Dough:
- In a small bowl, combine warm water, sugar, and active dry yeast. Let it sit for 5-10 minutes until frothy.
- In a large mixing bowl, combine the flour and salt. Make a well in the center and pour in the yeast mixture and olive oil.
- Mix until the dough comes together, then knead on a floured surface for 5-7 minutes or until smooth. Place the dough in an oiled bowl, cover with a damp cloth, and let it rise for 1-2 hours until doubled in size.

Preheat the Oven:

- Preheat your oven to the highest temperature it can go (typically around 475-500°F/245-260°C). If you have a pizza stone, place it in the oven during preheating.

Shape the Pizza Dough:
- Punch down the risen dough and transfer it to a floured surface. Roll it out into your desired pizza shape and thickness.

Assemble the Pizza:
- If using a pizza stone, transfer the rolled-out dough onto a pizza peel dusted with flour or cornmeal. If not using a stone, place the rolled-out dough on a lightly greased baking sheet.
- Spread an even layer of tomato sauce or pesto over the dough, leaving a small border around the edges.
- Sprinkle the shredded mozzarella cheese evenly over the sauce.
- Distribute the halved cherry tomatoes, sliced Kalamata olives, sliced artichoke hearts, and thinly sliced red onion over the pizza.
- Sprinkle crumbled feta cheese, chopped fresh basil, and capers (if using) over the top.
- Optionally, brush the crust with olive oil for a golden finish.

Bake the Pizza:
- If using a pizza stone, carefully transfer the pizza onto the preheated stone in the oven. If not using a stone, simply place the baking sheet in the oven.
- Bake for 10-12 minutes or until the crust is golden, the cheese is melted and bubbly, and the edges are slightly crispy.

Finish and Serve:
- Remove the pizza from the oven, let it cool for a few minutes, then slice and serve your mouthwatering Mediterranean Pizza!

Feel free to customize the toppings based on your preferences and add a drizzle of balsamic glaze or extra virgin olive oil for a finishing touch.

Mushroom and Truffle Oil Pizza

Ingredients:

Pizza Dough:

- 2 1/4 teaspoons (1 packet) active dry yeast
- 1 teaspoon sugar
- 3/4 cup warm water (110°F/43°C)
- 2 cups all-purpose flour
- 1 teaspoon salt
- 1 tablespoon olive oil

Truffle Oil Drizzle:

- 2 tablespoons truffle oil
- 1 tablespoon extra virgin olive oil

Pizza Toppings:

- 1 cup white or cremini mushrooms, thinly sliced
- 1 1/2 cups shredded mozzarella cheese
- 1/4 cup grated Parmesan cheese
- 1/4 cup caramelized onions (optional)
- Fresh thyme leaves
- Salt and black pepper to taste

Instructions:

Prepare the Pizza Dough:
- In a small bowl, combine warm water, sugar, and active dry yeast. Let it sit for 5-10 minutes until frothy.
- In a large mixing bowl, combine the flour and salt. Make a well in the center and pour in the yeast mixture and olive oil.
- Mix until the dough comes together, then knead on a floured surface for 5-7 minutes or until smooth. Place the dough in an oiled bowl, cover with a damp cloth, and let it rise for 1-2 hours until doubled in size.

Preheat the Oven:

- Preheat your oven to the highest temperature it can go (typically around 475-500°F/245-260°C). If you have a pizza stone, place it in the oven during preheating.

Shape the Pizza Dough:
- Punch down the risen dough and transfer it to a floured surface. Roll it out into your desired pizza shape and thickness.

Assemble the Pizza:
- If using a pizza stone, transfer the rolled-out dough onto a pizza peel dusted with flour or cornmeal. If not using a stone, place the rolled-out dough on a lightly greased baking sheet.
- Spread an even layer of shredded mozzarella cheese over the dough.
- Evenly distribute the thinly sliced mushrooms on top of the cheese.
- Optionally, add caramelized onions for added sweetness.
- Sprinkle grated Parmesan cheese over the pizza.
- Season with salt and black pepper to taste.
- Optionally, drizzle the truffle oil and extra virgin olive oil mixture over the pizza.
- Sprinkle fresh thyme leaves for added flavor.

Bake the Pizza:
- If using a pizza stone, carefully transfer the pizza onto the preheated stone in the oven. If not using a stone, simply place the baking sheet in the oven.
- Bake for 10-12 minutes or until the crust is golden, the cheese is melted and bubbly, and the edges are slightly crispy.

Finish and Serve:
- Remove the pizza from the oven, let it cool for a few minutes, then slice and serve your gourmet Mushroom and Truffle Oil Pizza!

Enjoy the rich and aromatic flavors of truffle oil combined with earthy mushrooms for a truly decadent pizza experience.

Caprese Pizza

Ingredients:

Pizza Dough:

- 2 1/4 teaspoons (1 packet) active dry yeast
- 1 teaspoon sugar
- 3/4 cup warm water (110°F/43°C)
- 2 cups all-purpose flour
- 1 teaspoon salt
- 1 tablespoon olive oil

Caprese Toppings:

- 1 cup pizza sauce (homemade or store-bought)
- 1 1/2 cups fresh mozzarella cheese, sliced or torn into pieces
- 2 medium tomatoes, thinly sliced
- Fresh basil leaves
- Balsamic glaze (store-bought or homemade)
- Salt and black pepper to taste
- Olive oil for brushing

Instructions:

   Prepare the Pizza Dough:
   - In a small bowl, combine warm water, sugar, and active dry yeast. Let it sit for 5-10 minutes until frothy.
   - In a large mixing bowl, combine the flour and salt. Make a well in the center and pour in the yeast mixture and olive oil.
   - Mix until the dough comes together, then knead on a floured surface for 5-7 minutes or until smooth. Place the dough in an oiled bowl, cover with a damp cloth, and let it rise for 1-2 hours until doubled in size.

   Preheat the Oven:
   - Preheat your oven to the highest temperature it can go (typically around 475-500°F/245-260°C). If you have a pizza stone, place it in the oven during preheating.

   Shape the Pizza Dough:

- Punch down the risen dough and transfer it to a floured surface. Roll it out into your desired pizza shape and thickness.

Assemble the Pizza:
- If using a pizza stone, transfer the rolled-out dough onto a pizza peel dusted with flour or cornmeal. If not using a stone, place the rolled-out dough on a lightly greased baking sheet.
- Spread an even layer of pizza sauce over the dough, leaving a small border around the edges.
- Arrange the sliced fresh mozzarella and tomato slices evenly over the sauce.
- Season with salt and black pepper to taste.
- Optionally, drizzle olive oil over the toppings.

Bake the Pizza:
- If using a pizza stone, carefully transfer the pizza onto the preheated stone in the oven. If not using a stone, simply place the baking sheet in the oven.
- Bake for 10-12 minutes or until the crust is golden, the cheese is melted and bubbly, and the edges are slightly crispy.

Finish and Serve:
- Remove the pizza from the oven, let it cool for a few minutes, then scatter fresh basil leaves over the top.
- Drizzle balsamic glaze over the pizza for added sweetness.
- Slice and serve your delicious Caprese Pizza!

Enjoy the fresh and vibrant flavors of a classic Caprese salad in pizza form. Customize it with your favorite variations, and savor the simplicity of this Italian-inspired dish.

Taco Pizza

Ingredients:

Pizza Dough:

- 2 1/4 teaspoons (1 packet) active dry yeast
- 1 teaspoon sugar
- 3/4 cup warm water (110°F/43°C)
- 2 cups all-purpose flour
- 1 teaspoon salt
- 1 tablespoon olive oil

Taco Seasoned Ground Beef:

- 1 pound ground beef
- 1 packet taco seasoning mix
- 1/2 cup water

Taco Pizza Toppings:

- 1 cup refried beans
- 1 cup shredded Mexican blend cheese
- 1 cup lettuce, shredded
- 1 cup tomatoes, diced
- 1/2 cup black olives, sliced
- 1/4 cup green onions, sliced
- 1/4 cup fresh cilantro, chopped
- Sour cream and salsa for serving

Instructions:

Prepare the Pizza Dough:
- In a small bowl, combine warm water, sugar, and active dry yeast. Let it sit for 5-10 minutes until frothy.
- In a large mixing bowl, combine the flour and salt. Make a well in the center and pour in the yeast mixture and olive oil.
- Mix until the dough comes together, then knead on a floured surface for 5-7 minutes or until smooth. Place the dough in an oiled bowl, cover with a damp cloth, and let it rise for 1-2 hours until doubled in size.

Preheat the Oven:
- Preheat your oven to the highest temperature it can go (typically around 475-500°F/245-260°C). If you have a pizza stone, place it in the oven during preheating.

Prepare Taco Seasoned Ground Beef:
- In a skillet over medium heat, brown the ground beef until fully cooked. Drain excess fat.
- Add the taco seasoning mix and water. Simmer for 5 minutes or until the mixture thickens. Set aside.

Shape the Pizza Dough:
- Punch down the risen dough and transfer it to a floured surface. Roll it out into your desired pizza shape and thickness.

Assemble the Taco Pizza:
- If using a pizza stone, transfer the rolled-out dough onto a pizza peel dusted with flour or cornmeal. If not using a stone, place the rolled-out dough on a lightly greased baking sheet.
- Spread an even layer of refried beans over the pizza dough.
- Evenly distribute the taco seasoned ground beef on top of the beans.
- Sprinkle shredded Mexican blend cheese over the beef.
- Bake in the preheated oven for 10-12 minutes or until the crust is golden and the cheese is melted and bubbly.

Add Fresh Toppings:
- Remove the pizza from the oven and top with shredded lettuce, diced tomatoes, sliced black olives, green onions, and chopped fresh cilantro.

Serve:
- Slice the Taco Pizza, and serve it hot with dollops of sour cream and salsa on the side.

Enjoy your Taco Pizza, combining the best of both worlds from tacos and pizza! Feel free to customize the toppings based on your preferences.

Greek Pizza

Ingredients:

Pizza Dough:

- 2 1/4 teaspoons (1 packet) active dry yeast
- 1 teaspoon sugar
- 3/4 cup warm water (110°F/43°C)
- 2 cups all-purpose flour
- 1 teaspoon salt
- 1 tablespoon olive oil

Greek Pizza Toppings:

- 1/2 cup tomato sauce or pesto (homemade or store-bought)
- 1 1/2 cups shredded mozzarella cheese
- 1/2 cup crumbled feta cheese
- 1/2 cup cherry tomatoes, halved
- 1/4 cup Kalamata olives, sliced
- 1/4 cup red onion, thinly sliced
- 1/4 cup artichoke hearts, drained and sliced
- 1/4 cup banana peppers or pepperoncini, sliced
- 1 tablespoon capers (optional)
- 1 teaspoon dried oregano
- Olive oil for brushing

Instructions:

Prepare the Pizza Dough:
- In a small bowl, combine warm water, sugar, and active dry yeast. Let it sit for 5-10 minutes until frothy.
- In a large mixing bowl, combine the flour and salt. Make a well in the center and pour in the yeast mixture and olive oil.
- Mix until the dough comes together, then knead on a floured surface for 5-7 minutes or until smooth. Place the dough in an oiled bowl, cover with a damp cloth, and let it rise for 1-2 hours until doubled in size.

Preheat the Oven:

- Preheat your oven to the highest temperature it can go (typically around 475-500°F/245-260°C). If you have a pizza stone, place it in the oven during preheating.

Shape the Pizza Dough:
- Punch down the risen dough and transfer it to a floured surface. Roll it out into your desired pizza shape and thickness.

Assemble the Greek Pizza:
- If using a pizza stone, transfer the rolled-out dough onto a pizza peel dusted with flour or cornmeal. If not using a stone, place the rolled-out dough on a lightly greased baking sheet.
- Spread an even layer of tomato sauce or pesto over the dough, leaving a small border around the edges.
- Sprinkle the shredded mozzarella cheese evenly over the sauce.
- Evenly distribute the crumbled feta cheese, halved cherry tomatoes, sliced Kalamata olives, thinly sliced red onion, sliced artichoke hearts, and sliced banana peppers or pepperoncini over the pizza.
- Sprinkle capers (if using) and dried oregano over the top.
- Optionally, brush the crust with olive oil for a golden finish.

Bake the Pizza:
- If using a pizza stone, carefully transfer the pizza onto the preheated stone in the oven. If not using a stone, simply place the baking sheet in the oven.
- Bake for 10-12 minutes or until the crust is golden, the cheese is melted and bubbly, and the edges are slightly crispy.

Finish and Serve:
- Remove the pizza from the oven, let it cool for a few minutes, then slice and serve your delightful Greek Pizza!

Enjoy the Mediterranean flavors of this Greek Pizza, and feel free to customize the toppings according to your taste preferences.

Shrimp Scampi Pizza

Ingredients:

Pizza Dough:

- 2 1/4 teaspoons (1 packet) active dry yeast
- 1 teaspoon sugar
- 3/4 cup warm water (110°F/43°C)
- 2 cups all-purpose flour
- 1 teaspoon salt
- 1 tablespoon olive oil

Shrimp Scampi Sauce:

- 3 tablespoons unsalted butter
- 3 tablespoons olive oil
- 4 cloves garlic, minced
- 1 pound large shrimp, peeled and deveined
- Salt and black pepper to taste
- 1/4 teaspoon red pepper flakes (optional)
- 1/4 cup fresh parsley, chopped
- 1 tablespoon lemon juice

Pizza Toppings:

- 1 1/2 cups shredded mozzarella cheese
- 1/4 cup grated Parmesan cheese
- 1 tablespoon lemon zest
- Fresh parsley, chopped, for garnish

Instructions:

Prepare the Pizza Dough:
- In a small bowl, combine warm water, sugar, and active dry yeast. Let it sit for 5-10 minutes until frothy.
- In a large mixing bowl, combine the flour and salt. Make a well in the center and pour in the yeast mixture and olive oil.

- Mix until the dough comes together, then knead on a floured surface for 5-7 minutes or until smooth. Place the dough in an oiled bowl, cover with a damp cloth, and let it rise for 1-2 hours until doubled in size.

Prepare the Shrimp Scampi Sauce:
- In a large skillet, melt butter and olive oil over medium heat.
- Add minced garlic and sauté for 1-2 minutes until fragrant.
- Add shrimp to the skillet, season with salt, black pepper, and red pepper flakes (if using). Cook until the shrimp turn pink and opaque.
- Stir in chopped parsley and lemon juice. Remove from heat and set aside.

Preheat the Oven:
- Preheat your oven to the highest temperature it can go (typically around 475-500°F/245-260°C). If you have a pizza stone, place it in the oven during preheating.

Shape the Pizza Dough:
- Punch down the risen dough and transfer it to a floured surface. Roll it out into your desired pizza shape and thickness.

Assemble the Shrimp Scampi Pizza:
- If using a pizza stone, transfer the rolled-out dough onto a pizza peel dusted with flour or cornmeal. If not using a stone, place the rolled-out dough on a lightly greased baking sheet.
- Spread an even layer of shredded mozzarella cheese over the dough.
- Evenly distribute the shrimp scampi mixture over the cheese.
- Sprinkle grated Parmesan cheese over the top.
- Optionally, add lemon zest for extra freshness.

Bake the Pizza:
- If using a pizza stone, carefully transfer the pizza onto the preheated stone in the oven. If not using a stone, simply place the baking sheet in the oven.
- Bake for 10-12 minutes or until the crust is golden, the cheese is melted and bubbly, and the edges are slightly crispy.

Finish and Serve:
- Remove the pizza from the oven, let it cool for a few minutes, then garnish with chopped fresh parsley.
- Slice and serve your delicious Shrimp Scampi Pizza!

Enjoy the succulent shrimp scampi flavors on a pizza crust for a delightful seafood twist!

Breakfast Pizza

Ingredients:

Pizza Dough:

- 2 1/4 teaspoons (1 packet) active dry yeast
- 1 teaspoon sugar
- 3/4 cup warm water (110°F/43°C)
- 2 cups all-purpose flour
- 1 teaspoon salt
- 1 tablespoon olive oil

Breakfast Pizza Toppings:

- 1 cup shredded mozzarella cheese
- 4 large eggs
- Salt and black pepper to taste
- 4 slices bacon, cooked and crumbled
- 1/2 cup diced bell peppers
- 1/2 cup diced onions
- 1/2 cup diced tomatoes
- 1/4 cup chopped fresh parsley or chives
- Optional toppings: cooked sausage, mushrooms, spinach, feta cheese, hot sauce

Instructions:

Prepare the Pizza Dough:
- In a small bowl, combine warm water, sugar, and active dry yeast. Let it sit for 5-10 minutes until frothy.
- In a large mixing bowl, combine the flour and salt. Make a well in the center and pour in the yeast mixture and olive oil.
- Mix until the dough comes together, then knead on a floured surface for 5-7 minutes or until smooth. Place the dough in an oiled bowl, cover with a damp cloth, and let it rise for 1-2 hours until doubled in size.

Preheat the Oven:
- Preheat your oven to the highest temperature it can go (typically around 475-500°F/245-260°C). If you have a pizza stone, place it in the oven during preheating.

Shape the Pizza Dough:
- Punch down the risen dough and transfer it to a floured surface. Roll it out into your desired pizza shape and thickness.

Assemble the Breakfast Pizza:
- If using a pizza stone, transfer the rolled-out dough onto a pizza peel dusted with flour or cornmeal. If not using a stone, place the rolled-out dough on a lightly greased baking sheet.
- Sprinkle shredded mozzarella cheese evenly over the dough, leaving a small border around the edges.
- Create wells in the cheese for the eggs. Crack an egg into each well.
- Season the eggs with salt and black pepper to taste.
- Distribute crumbled bacon, diced bell peppers, diced onions, diced tomatoes, and any other desired toppings over the pizza.

Bake the Pizza:
- If using a pizza stone, carefully transfer the pizza onto the preheated stone in the oven. If not using a stone, simply place the baking sheet in the oven.
- Bake for 12-15 minutes or until the crust is golden, the cheese is melted, and the eggs are cooked to your liking.

Finish and Serve:
- Remove the pizza from the oven, sprinkle chopped fresh parsley or chives over the top.
- Slice and serve your delicious Breakfast Pizza!

Feel free to get creative with your toppings and customize the pizza to suit your breakfast preferences. Enjoy your homemade breakfast pizza!

Fig and Prosciutto Pizza

Ingredients:

Pizza Dough:

- 2 1/4 teaspoons (1 packet) active dry yeast
- 1 teaspoon sugar
- 3/4 cup warm water (110°F/43°C)
- 2 cups all-purpose flour
- 1 teaspoon salt
- 1 tablespoon olive oil

Fig and Prosciutto Toppings:

- 1/2 cup fig jam
- 1 1/2 cups shredded mozzarella cheese
- 4-6 slices prosciutto
- 1/2 cup crumbled goat cheese
- 1/4 cup chopped walnuts
- Fresh arugula for topping
- Balsamic glaze for drizzling (optional)
- Olive oil for brushing

Instructions:

Prepare the Pizza Dough:
- In a small bowl, combine warm water, sugar, and active dry yeast. Let it sit for 5-10 minutes until frothy.
- In a large mixing bowl, combine the flour and salt. Make a well in the center and pour in the yeast mixture and olive oil.
- Mix until the dough comes together, then knead on a floured surface for 5-7 minutes or until smooth. Place the dough in an oiled bowl, cover with a damp cloth, and let it rise for 1-2 hours until doubled in size.

Preheat the Oven:
- Preheat your oven to the highest temperature it can go (typically around 475-500°F/245-260°C). If you have a pizza stone, place it in the oven during preheating.

Shape the Pizza Dough:

- Punch down the risen dough and transfer it to a floured surface. Roll it out into your desired pizza shape and thickness.

Assemble the Fig and Prosciutto Pizza:
- If using a pizza stone, transfer the rolled-out dough onto a pizza peel dusted with flour or cornmeal. If not using a stone, place the rolled-out dough on a lightly greased baking sheet.
- Spread an even layer of fig jam over the pizza dough, leaving a small border around the edges.
- Sprinkle shredded mozzarella cheese evenly over the fig jam.
- Arrange prosciutto slices on top of the cheese.
- Crumble goat cheese over the pizza and sprinkle chopped walnuts.
- Optionally, brush the crust with olive oil for a golden finish.

Bake the Pizza:
- If using a pizza stone, carefully transfer the pizza onto the preheated stone in the oven. If not using a stone, simply place the baking sheet in the oven.
- Bake for 10-12 minutes or until the crust is golden, the cheese is melted and bubbly, and the edges are slightly crispy.

Finish and Serve:
- Remove the pizza from the oven, let it cool for a few minutes, then top with fresh arugula.
- Optionally, drizzle balsamic glaze over the top for added sweetness.
- Slice and serve your elegant Fig and Prosciutto Pizza!

Enjoy the rich and harmonious flavors of fig, prosciutto, and goat cheese in this gourmet pizza creation.

Philly Cheesesteak Pizza

Ingredients:

Pizza Dough:

- 2 1/4 teaspoons (1 packet) active dry yeast
- 1 teaspoon sugar
- 3/4 cup warm water (110°F/43°C)
- 2 cups all-purpose flour
- 1 teaspoon salt
- 1 tablespoon olive oil

Philly Cheesesteak Toppings:

- 1 pound ribeye steak, thinly sliced
- Salt and black pepper to taste
- 1 tablespoon vegetable oil
- 1 green bell pepper, thinly sliced
- 1 onion, thinly sliced
- 1 cup shredded provolone cheese
- 1 cup shredded mozzarella cheese
- 1/4 cup mayonnaise
- 2 tablespoons Dijon mustard (optional)
- Fresh parsley, chopped, for garnish

Instructions:

Prepare the Pizza Dough:
- In a small bowl, combine warm water, sugar, and active dry yeast. Let it sit for 5-10 minutes until frothy.
- In a large mixing bowl, combine the flour and salt. Make a well in the center and pour in the yeast mixture and olive oil.
- Mix until the dough comes together, then knead on a floured surface for 5-7 minutes or until smooth. Place the dough in an oiled bowl, cover with a damp cloth, and let it rise for 1-2 hours until doubled in size.

Preheat the Oven:
- Preheat your oven to the highest temperature it can go (typically around 475-500°F/245-260°C). If you have a pizza stone, place it in the oven during preheating.

Prepare Philly Cheesesteak Toppings:
- Season the thinly sliced ribeye steak with salt and black pepper.
- In a skillet over medium-high heat, heat vegetable oil. Sear the sliced steak until cooked to your liking. Remove the steak from the skillet and set aside.
- In the same skillet, add a bit more oil if needed, and sauté the sliced green bell pepper and onion until softened.

Shape the Pizza Dough:
- Punch down the risen dough and transfer it to a floured surface. Roll it out into your desired pizza shape and thickness.

Assemble the Philly Cheesesteak Pizza:
- If using a pizza stone, transfer the rolled-out dough onto a pizza peel dusted with flour or cornmeal. If not using a stone, place the rolled-out dough on a lightly greased baking sheet.
- Spread an even layer of shredded provolone cheese over the pizza dough.
- Arrange the cooked ribeye steak, sautéed bell pepper, and onion evenly over the cheese.
- Sprinkle shredded mozzarella cheese on top.
- Optionally, drizzle mayonnaise and Dijon mustard (if using) over the pizza.

Bake the Pizza:
- If using a pizza stone, carefully transfer the pizza onto the preheated stone in the oven. If not using a stone, simply place the baking sheet in the oven.
- Bake for 10-12 minutes or until the crust is golden, the cheese is melted and bubbly, and the edges are slightly crispy.

Finish and Serve:
- Remove the pizza from the oven, let it cool for a few minutes, then sprinkle chopped fresh parsley over the top.
- Slice and serve your delicious Philly Cheesesteak Pizza!

Enjoy the savory and satisfying flavors of a Philly cheesesteak in pizza form. Customize with your favorite toppings and savor this fusion of two beloved dishes.

Chicken Alfredo Pizza

Ingredients:

Pizza Dough:

- 2 1/4 teaspoons (1 packet) active dry yeast
- 1 teaspoon sugar
- 3/4 cup warm water (110°F/43°C)
- 2 cups all-purpose flour
- 1 teaspoon salt
- 1 tablespoon olive oil

Chicken Alfredo Sauce:

- 1 cup Alfredo sauce (homemade or store-bought)
- 2 cups cooked chicken breast, shredded or diced
- 1 cup shredded mozzarella cheese
- 1/2 cup grated Parmesan cheese
- 2 cloves garlic, minced
- Salt and black pepper to taste
- 1 tablespoon fresh parsley, chopped

Additional Toppings:

- Sliced mushrooms
- Baby spinach leaves
- Cherry tomatoes, halved
- Red onion, thinly sliced

Instructions:

Prepare the Pizza Dough:
- In a small bowl, combine warm water, sugar, and active dry yeast. Let it sit for 5-10 minutes until frothy.
- In a large mixing bowl, combine the flour and salt. Make a well in the center and pour in the yeast mixture and olive oil.
- Mix until the dough comes together, then knead on a floured surface for 5-7 minutes or until smooth. Place the dough in an oiled bowl, cover with a damp cloth, and let it rise for 1-2 hours until doubled in size.

Preheat the Oven:
- Preheat your oven to the highest temperature it can go (typically around 475-500°F/245-260°C). If you have a pizza stone, place it in the oven during preheating.

Prepare Chicken Alfredo Sauce:
- In a bowl, mix Alfredo sauce, minced garlic, salt, and black pepper. Set aside.

Shape the Pizza Dough:
- Punch down the risen dough and transfer it to a floured surface. Roll it out into your desired pizza shape and thickness.

Assemble Chicken Alfredo Pizza:
- If using a pizza stone, transfer the rolled-out dough onto a pizza peel dusted with flour or cornmeal. If not using a stone, place the rolled-out dough on a lightly greased baking sheet.
- Spread an even layer of the prepared Chicken Alfredo sauce over the pizza dough, leaving a small border around the edges.
- Evenly distribute the cooked chicken over the sauce.
- Sprinkle shredded mozzarella cheese and grated Parmesan cheese over the pizza.
- Add additional toppings like sliced mushrooms, baby spinach leaves, cherry tomatoes, and thinly sliced red onion.

Bake the Pizza:
- If using a pizza stone, carefully transfer the pizza onto the preheated stone in the oven. If not using a stone, simply place the baking sheet in the oven.
- Bake for 10-12 minutes or until the crust is golden, the cheese is melted and bubbly, and the edges are slightly crispy.

Finish and Serve:
- Remove the pizza from the oven, let it cool for a few minutes, then sprinkle chopped fresh parsley over the top.
- Slice and serve your creamy and flavorful Chicken Alfredo Pizza!

Enjoy the indulgent flavors of Alfredo sauce, chicken, and your favorite toppings on a homemade pizza crust. Customize it to your liking and savor this delicious fusion of pizza and pasta.

Artichoke and Olive Pizza

Ingredients:

Pizza Dough:

- 2 1/4 teaspoons (1 packet) active dry yeast
- 1 teaspoon sugar
- 3/4 cup warm water (110°F/43°C)
- 2 cups all-purpose flour
- 1 teaspoon salt
- 1 tablespoon olive oil

Artichoke and Olive Toppings:

- 1 cup pizza sauce (homemade or store-bought)
- 1 1/2 cups shredded mozzarella cheese
- 1 cup marinated artichoke hearts, drained and quartered
- 1/2 cup Kalamata olives, sliced
- 1/4 cup black olives, sliced
- 1/4 cup red onion, thinly sliced
- 1/4 cup feta cheese, crumbled
- 1 tablespoon fresh oregano or basil, chopped
- Olive oil for brushing

Instructions:

Prepare the Pizza Dough:
- In a small bowl, combine warm water, sugar, and active dry yeast. Let it sit for 5-10 minutes until frothy.
- In a large mixing bowl, combine the flour and salt. Make a well in the center and pour in the yeast mixture and olive oil.
- Mix until the dough comes together, then knead on a floured surface for 5-7 minutes or until smooth. Place the dough in an oiled bowl, cover with a damp cloth, and let it rise for 1-2 hours until doubled in size.

Preheat the Oven:
- Preheat your oven to the highest temperature it can go (typically around 475-500°F/245-260°C). If you have a pizza stone, place it in the oven during preheating.

Shape the Pizza Dough:
- Punch down the risen dough and transfer it to a floured surface. Roll it out into your desired pizza shape and thickness.

Assemble Artichoke and Olive Pizza:
- If using a pizza stone, transfer the rolled-out dough onto a pizza peel dusted with flour or cornmeal. If not using a stone, place the rolled-out dough on a lightly greased baking sheet.
- Spread an even layer of pizza sauce over the dough, leaving a small border around the edges.
- Sprinkle shredded mozzarella cheese evenly over the sauce.
- Distribute quartered artichoke hearts, sliced Kalamata olives, sliced black olives, and thinly sliced red onion over the pizza.
- Sprinkle crumbled feta cheese over the toppings.
- Optionally, brush the crust with olive oil for a golden finish.

Bake the Pizza:
- If using a pizza stone, carefully transfer the pizza onto the preheated stone in the oven. If not using a stone, simply place the baking sheet in the oven.
- Bake for 10-12 minutes or until the crust is golden, the cheese is melted and bubbly, and the edges are slightly crispy.

Finish and Serve:
- Remove the pizza from the oven, let it cool for a few minutes, then sprinkle fresh oregano or basil over the top.
- Slice and serve your delicious Artichoke and Olive Pizza!

Enjoy the Mediterranean-inspired flavors of artichokes and olives on this flavorful homemade pizza. Customize it with your favorite ingredients and savor the unique combination of tastes.

Spinach and Feta Pizza

Ingredients:

Pizza Dough:

- 2 1/4 teaspoons (1 packet) active dry yeast
- 1 teaspoon sugar
- 3/4 cup warm water (110°F/43°C)
- 2 cups all-purpose flour
- 1 teaspoon salt
- 1 tablespoon olive oil

Spinach and Feta Toppings:

- 1 cup pizza sauce (homemade or store-bought)
- 1 1/2 cups shredded mozzarella cheese
- 2 cups fresh spinach leaves, washed and dried
- 1 cup crumbled feta cheese
- 1/4 cup red onion, thinly sliced
- 1 clove garlic, minced
- 1/4 teaspoon red pepper flakes (optional)
- Olive oil for brushing

Instructions:

Prepare the Pizza Dough:
- In a small bowl, combine warm water, sugar, and active dry yeast. Let it sit for 5-10 minutes until frothy.
- In a large mixing bowl, combine the flour and salt. Make a well in the center and pour in the yeast mixture and olive oil.
- Mix until the dough comes together, then knead on a floured surface for 5-7 minutes or until smooth. Place the dough in an oiled bowl, cover with a damp cloth, and let it rise for 1-2 hours until doubled in size.

Preheat the Oven:
- Preheat your oven to the highest temperature it can go (typically around 475-500°F/245-260°C). If you have a pizza stone, place it in the oven during preheating.

Shape the Pizza Dough:

- Punch down the risen dough and transfer it to a floured surface. Roll it out into your desired pizza shape and thickness.

Assemble Spinach and Feta Pizza:
- If using a pizza stone, transfer the rolled-out dough onto a pizza peel dusted with flour or cornmeal. If not using a stone, place the rolled-out dough on a lightly greased baking sheet.
- Spread an even layer of pizza sauce over the dough, leaving a small border around the edges.
- Sprinkle shredded mozzarella cheese evenly over the sauce.
- Distribute fresh spinach leaves, crumbled feta cheese, thinly sliced red onion, minced garlic, and red pepper flakes (if using) over the pizza.
- Optionally, brush the crust with olive oil for a golden finish.

Bake the Pizza:
- If using a pizza stone, carefully transfer the pizza onto the preheated stone in the oven. If not using a stone, simply place the baking sheet in the oven.
- Bake for 10-12 minutes or until the crust is golden, the cheese is melted and bubbly, and the edges are slightly crispy.

Finish and Serve:
- Remove the pizza from the oven, let it cool for a few minutes, then slice and serve your delicious Spinach and Feta Pizza!

Enjoy the vibrant and savory flavors of spinach and feta in this simple and tasty homemade pizza. Customize it with additional toppings if desired, and savor every bite.

Roasted Red Pepper and Goat Cheese Pizza

Ingredients:

Pizza Dough:

- 2 1/4 teaspoons (1 packet) active dry yeast
- 1 teaspoon sugar
- 3/4 cup warm water (110°F/43°C)
- 2 cups all-purpose flour
- 1 teaspoon salt
- 1 tablespoon olive oil

Roasted Red Pepper and Goat Cheese Toppings:

- 1 cup pizza sauce (homemade or store-bought)
- 1 1/2 cups shredded mozzarella cheese
- 1 cup crumbled goat cheese
- 1 cup roasted red peppers, sliced (you can use jarred or roast them yourself)
- 1/4 cup red onion, thinly sliced
- 1/4 cup pine nuts
- Fresh basil, chopped, for garnish
- Olive oil for brushing

Instructions:

Prepare the Pizza Dough:
- In a small bowl, combine warm water, sugar, and active dry yeast. Let it sit for 5-10 minutes until frothy.
- In a large mixing bowl, combine the flour and salt. Make a well in the center and pour in the yeast mixture and olive oil.
- Mix until the dough comes together, then knead on a floured surface for 5-7 minutes or until smooth. Place the dough in an oiled bowl, cover with a damp cloth, and let it rise for 1-2 hours until doubled in size.

Preheat the Oven:
- Preheat your oven to the highest temperature it can go (typically around 475-500°F/245-260°C). If you have a pizza stone, place it in the oven during preheating.

Shape the Pizza Dough:

- Punch down the risen dough and transfer it to a floured surface. Roll it out into your desired pizza shape and thickness.

Assemble Roasted Red Pepper and Goat Cheese Pizza:
- If using a pizza stone, transfer the rolled-out dough onto a pizza peel dusted with flour or cornmeal. If not using a stone, place the rolled-out dough on a lightly greased baking sheet.
- Spread an even layer of pizza sauce over the dough, leaving a small border around the edges.
- Sprinkle shredded mozzarella cheese evenly over the sauce.
- Distribute sliced roasted red peppers, crumbled goat cheese, and thinly sliced red onion over the pizza.
- Sprinkle pine nuts over the toppings.
- Optionally, brush the crust with olive oil for a golden finish.

Bake the Pizza:
- If using a pizza stone, carefully transfer the pizza onto the preheated stone in the oven. If not using a stone, simply place the baking sheet in the oven.
- Bake for 10-12 minutes or until the crust is golden, the cheese is melted and bubbly, and the edges are slightly crispy.

Finish and Serve:
- Remove the pizza from the oven, let it cool for a few minutes, then sprinkle chopped fresh basil over the top.
- Slice and serve your delightful Roasted Red Pepper and Goat Cheese Pizza!

Enjoy the unique combination of sweet roasted red peppers and tangy goat cheese on this flavorful homemade pizza. Customize it to your liking and savor the delicious medley of tastes.

BLT Pizza

Ingredients:

Pizza Dough:

- 2 1/4 teaspoons (1 packet) active dry yeast
- 1 teaspoon sugar
- 3/4 cup warm water (110°F/43°C)
- 2 cups all-purpose flour
- 1 teaspoon salt
- 1 tablespoon olive oil

BLT Toppings:

- 1 cup pizza sauce (homemade or store-bought)
- 1 1/2 cups shredded mozzarella cheese
- 8 slices bacon, cooked and crumbled
- 1 cup cherry tomatoes, halved
- 1 cup iceberg lettuce, shredded
- 1/4 cup mayonnaise
- 1 teaspoon Dijon mustard
- Salt and black pepper to taste
- Fresh parsley, chopped, for garnish

Instructions:

Prepare the Pizza Dough:
- In a small bowl, combine warm water, sugar, and active dry yeast. Let it sit for 5-10 minutes until frothy.
- In a large mixing bowl, combine the flour and salt. Make a well in the center and pour in the yeast mixture and olive oil.
- Mix until the dough comes together, then knead on a floured surface for 5-7 minutes or until smooth. Place the dough in an oiled bowl, cover with a damp cloth, and let it rise for 1-2 hours until doubled in size.

Preheat the Oven:
- Preheat your oven to the highest temperature it can go (typically around 475-500°F/245-260°C). If you have a pizza stone, place it in the oven during preheating.

Shape the Pizza Dough:
- Punch down the risen dough and transfer it to a floured surface. Roll it out into your desired pizza shape and thickness.

Assemble BLT Pizza:
- If using a pizza stone, transfer the rolled-out dough onto a pizza peel dusted with flour or cornmeal. If not using a stone, place the rolled-out dough on a lightly greased baking sheet.
- Spread an even layer of pizza sauce over the dough, leaving a small border around the edges.
- Sprinkle shredded mozzarella cheese evenly over the sauce.
- Distribute crumbled bacon and halved cherry tomatoes over the pizza.

Bake the Pizza:
- If using a pizza stone, carefully transfer the pizza onto the preheated stone in the oven. If not using a stone, simply place the baking sheet in the oven.
- Bake for 10-12 minutes or until the crust is golden, the cheese is melted and bubbly, and the edges are slightly crispy.

Prepare the Toppings:
- While the pizza is baking, mix mayonnaise and Dijon mustard in a small bowl. Season with salt and black pepper to taste.

Finish and Serve:
- Remove the pizza from the oven, let it cool for a few minutes, then drizzle the mayonnaise mixture over the top.
- Sprinkle shredded iceberg lettuce on the pizza.
- Optionally, garnish with chopped fresh parsley.
- Slice and serve your tasty BLT Pizza!

Enjoy the classic combination of bacon, lettuce, and tomato on a pizza crust, creating a delicious fusion of flavors. Customize it with your preferred pizza sauce and cheese for a personalized twist.

Caramelized Onion and Gorgonzola Pizza

Ingredients:

Pizza Dough:

- 2 1/4 teaspoons (1 packet) active dry yeast
- 1 teaspoon sugar
- 3/4 cup warm water (110°F/43°C)
- 2 cups all-purpose flour
- 1 teaspoon salt
- 1 tablespoon olive oil

Caramelized Onion and Gorgonzola Toppings:

- 2 large onions, thinly sliced
- 2 tablespoons butter
- 1 tablespoon olive oil
- Salt and black pepper to taste
- 1 cup Gorgonzola cheese, crumbled
- 1 1/2 cups shredded mozzarella cheese
- 1 tablespoon balsamic glaze (optional)
- Fresh thyme or rosemary, chopped, for garnish

Instructions:

Prepare the Pizza Dough:
- In a small bowl, combine warm water, sugar, and active dry yeast. Let it sit for 5-10 minutes until frothy.
- In a large mixing bowl, combine the flour and salt. Make a well in the center and pour in the yeast mixture and olive oil.
- Mix until the dough comes together, then knead on a floured surface for 5-7 minutes or until smooth. Place the dough in an oiled bowl, cover with a damp cloth, and let it rise for 1-2 hours until doubled in size.

Preheat the Oven:
- Preheat your oven to the highest temperature it can go (typically around 475-500°F/245-260°C). If you have a pizza stone, place it in the oven during preheating.

Caramelize the Onions:

- In a skillet over medium-low heat, melt butter and olive oil. Add thinly sliced onions and cook slowly, stirring occasionally, until the onions are soft, golden brown, and caramelized. Season with salt and black pepper. This may take about 20-30 minutes.

Shape the Pizza Dough:
- Punch down the risen dough and transfer it to a floured surface. Roll it out into your desired pizza shape and thickness.

Assemble Caramelized Onion and Gorgonzola Pizza:
- If using a pizza stone, transfer the rolled-out dough onto a pizza peel dusted with flour or cornmeal. If not using a stone, place the rolled-out dough on a lightly greased baking sheet.
- Spread an even layer of caramelized onions over the dough, leaving a small border around the edges.
- Sprinkle shredded mozzarella cheese evenly over the onions.
- Distribute crumbled Gorgonzola cheese over the pizza.

Bake the Pizza:
- If using a pizza stone, carefully transfer the pizza onto the preheated stone in the oven. If not using a stone, simply place the baking sheet in the oven.
- Bake for 10-12 minutes or until the crust is golden, the cheese is melted and bubbly, and the edges are slightly crispy.

Finish and Serve:
- Remove the pizza from the oven, drizzle with balsamic glaze (if using), and sprinkle chopped fresh thyme or rosemary over the top.
- Slice and serve your delicious Caramelized Onion and Gorgonzola Pizza!

Enjoy the rich and savory flavors of caramelized onions and Gorgonzola on this homemade pizza. The balsamic glaze adds a touch of sweetness, creating a perfect balance of tastes.

Thai Chicken Pizza

Ingredients:

Pizza Dough:

- 2 1/4 teaspoons (1 packet) active dry yeast
- 1 teaspoon sugar
- 3/4 cup warm water (110°F/43°C)
- 2 cups all-purpose flour
- 1 teaspoon salt
- 1 tablespoon olive oil

Thai Chicken Toppings:

- 1 cup cooked and shredded chicken breast
- 1/2 cup peanut sauce (store-bought or homemade)
- 1 cup shredded mozzarella cheese
- 1/2 cup shredded carrots
- 1/2 cup red bell pepper, thinly sliced
- 1/4 cup red onion, thinly sliced
- 1/4 cup chopped cilantro
- 1/4 cup chopped green onions
- Crushed red pepper flakes (optional)
- Lime wedges for serving

Instructions:

Prepare the Pizza Dough:
- In a small bowl, combine warm water, sugar, and active dry yeast. Let it sit for 5-10 minutes until frothy.
- In a large mixing bowl, combine the flour and salt. Make a well in the center and pour in the yeast mixture and olive oil.
- Mix until the dough comes together, then knead on a floured surface for 5-7 minutes or until smooth. Place the dough in an oiled bowl, cover with a damp cloth, and let it rise for 1-2 hours until doubled in size.

Preheat the Oven:

- Preheat your oven to the highest temperature it can go (typically around 475-500°F/245-260°C). If you have a pizza stone, place it in the oven during preheating.

Shape the Pizza Dough:
- Punch down the risen dough and transfer it to a floured surface. Roll it out into your desired pizza shape and thickness.

Assemble Thai Chicken Pizza:
- If using a pizza stone, transfer the rolled-out dough onto a pizza peel dusted with flour or cornmeal. If not using a stone, place the rolled-out dough on a lightly greased baking sheet.
- Spread an even layer of peanut sauce over the dough, leaving a small border around the edges.
- Sprinkle shredded mozzarella cheese evenly over the peanut sauce.
- Distribute shredded chicken, shredded carrots, sliced red bell pepper, and sliced red onion over the pizza.

Bake the Pizza:
- If using a pizza stone, carefully transfer the pizza onto the preheated stone in the oven. If not using a stone, simply place the baking sheet in the oven.
- Bake for 10-12 minutes or until the crust is golden, the cheese is melted and bubbly, and the edges are slightly crispy.

Finish and Serve:
- Remove the pizza from the oven, sprinkle chopped cilantro and green onions over the top.
- Optionally, add a sprinkle of crushed red pepper flakes for extra heat.
- Slice and serve your flavorful Thai Chicken Pizza with lime wedges on the side.

Enjoy the bold and zesty flavors of Thai cuisine on a pizza crust. This fusion dish is a crowd-pleaser and offers a unique twist to traditional pizza.

Clam and Garlic Pizza

Ingredients:

Pizza Dough:

- 2 1/4 teaspoons (1 packet) active dry yeast
- 1 teaspoon sugar
- 3/4 cup warm water (110°F/43°C)
- 2 cups all-purpose flour
- 1 teaspoon salt
- 1 tablespoon olive oil

Clam and Garlic Toppings:

- 1 cup canned minced clams, drained
- 3 tablespoons olive oil
- 4 cloves garlic, minced
- 1/4 teaspoon red pepper flakes (optional)
- 1 cup shredded mozzarella cheese
- 1/4 cup grated Parmesan cheese
- 2 tablespoons fresh parsley, chopped
- Lemon wedges for serving

Instructions:

Prepare the Pizza Dough:
- In a small bowl, combine warm water, sugar, and active dry yeast. Let it sit for 5-10 minutes until frothy.
- In a large mixing bowl, combine the flour and salt. Make a well in the center and pour in the yeast mixture and olive oil.
- Mix until the dough comes together, then knead on a floured surface for 5-7 minutes or until smooth. Place the dough in an oiled bowl, cover with a damp cloth, and let it rise for 1-2 hours until doubled in size.

Preheat the Oven:
- Preheat your oven to the highest temperature it can go (typically around 475-500°F/245-260°C). If you have a pizza stone, place it in the oven during preheating.

Shape the Pizza Dough:

- Punch down the risen dough and transfer it to a floured surface. Roll it out into your desired pizza shape and thickness.

Prepare the Clam and Garlic Toppings:
- In a small bowl, mix minced clams with 1 tablespoon of olive oil. Set aside.
- In a separate skillet, heat 2 tablespoons of olive oil over medium heat. Add minced garlic and red pepper flakes (if using) and sauté for about 1-2 minutes until fragrant.

Assemble Clam and Garlic Pizza:
- If using a pizza stone, transfer the rolled-out dough onto a pizza peel dusted with flour or cornmeal. If not using a stone, place the rolled-out dough on a lightly greased baking sheet.
- Spread the sautéed garlic evenly over the pizza dough.
- Distribute the clam and olive oil mixture evenly over the garlic.
- Sprinkle shredded mozzarella cheese and grated Parmesan cheese over the pizza.

Bake the Pizza:
- If using a pizza stone, carefully transfer the pizza onto the preheated stone in the oven. If not using a stone, simply place the baking sheet in the oven.
- Bake for 10-12 minutes or until the crust is golden, the cheese is melted and bubbly, and the edges are slightly crispy.

Finish and Serve:
- Remove the pizza from the oven, sprinkle chopped fresh parsley over the top.
- Serve your Clam and Garlic Pizza with lemon wedges on the side for a citrusy kick.

Enjoy the distinct flavors of clams and garlic on this delectable homemade pizza. The addition of lemon wedges enhances the seafood taste, making it a delightful and refreshing choice.

Sun-Dried Tomato and Basil Pizza

Ingredients:

Pizza Dough:

- 2 1/4 teaspoons (1 packet) active dry yeast
- 1 teaspoon sugar
- 3/4 cup warm water (110°F/43°C)
- 2 cups all-purpose flour
- 1 teaspoon salt
- 1 tablespoon olive oil

Sun-Dried Tomato and Basil Toppings:

- 1/2 cup pizza sauce (homemade or store-bought)
- 1 1/2 cups shredded mozzarella cheese
- 1/2 cup sun-dried tomatoes, rehydrated and sliced
- 1/4 cup Kalamata olives, sliced
- 1/4 cup red onion, thinly sliced
- 1/4 cup fresh basil leaves, torn
- 2 tablespoons pine nuts
- 1/4 cup grated Parmesan cheese
- Olive oil for brushing

Instructions:

Prepare the Pizza Dough:
- In a small bowl, combine warm water, sugar, and active dry yeast. Let it sit for 5-10 minutes until frothy.
- In a large mixing bowl, combine the flour and salt. Make a well in the center and pour in the yeast mixture and olive oil.
- Mix until the dough comes together, then knead on a floured surface for 5-7 minutes or until smooth. Place the dough in an oiled bowl, cover with a damp cloth, and let it rise for 1-2 hours until doubled in size.

Preheat the Oven:
- Preheat your oven to the highest temperature it can go (typically around 475-500°F/245-260°C). If you have a pizza stone, place it in the oven during preheating.

Rehydrate Sun-Dried Tomatoes:
- Place the sun-dried tomatoes in a bowl of warm water and let them soak for about 15-20 minutes until they become plump. Drain and slice them.

Shape the Pizza Dough:
- Punch down the risen dough and transfer it to a floured surface. Roll it out into your desired pizza shape and thickness.

Assemble Sun-Dried Tomato and Basil Pizza:
- If using a pizza stone, transfer the rolled-out dough onto a pizza peel dusted with flour or cornmeal. If not using a stone, place the rolled-out dough on a lightly greased baking sheet.
- Spread an even layer of pizza sauce over the dough, leaving a small border around the edges.
- Sprinkle shredded mozzarella cheese evenly over the sauce.
- Distribute rehydrated and sliced sun-dried tomatoes, sliced Kalamata olives, thinly sliced red onion, and torn fresh basil leaves over the pizza.
- Sprinkle pine nuts and grated Parmesan cheese over the toppings.
- Optionally, brush the crust with olive oil for a golden finish.

Bake the Pizza:
- If using a pizza stone, carefully transfer the pizza onto the preheated stone in the oven. If not using a stone, simply place the baking sheet in the oven.
- Bake for 10-12 minutes or until the crust is golden, the cheese is melted and bubbly, and the edges are slightly crispy.

Finish and Serve:
- Remove the pizza from the oven, let it cool for a few minutes, then slice and serve your delicious Sun-Dried Tomato and Basil Pizza!

Enjoy the vibrant flavors of sun-dried tomatoes and fresh basil on this homemade pizza. The combination of sweet, savory, and herby notes creates a perfect harmony of tastes.

Buffalo Cauliflower Pizza

Ingredients:

Pizza Dough:

- 2 1/4 teaspoons (1 packet) active dry yeast
- 1 teaspoon sugar
- 3/4 cup warm water (110°F/43°C)
- 2 cups all-purpose flour
- 1 teaspoon salt
- 1 tablespoon olive oil

Buffalo Cauliflower Toppings:

- 3 cups cauliflower florets, cut into bite-sized pieces
- 2 tablespoons olive oil
- Salt and black pepper to taste
- 1/2 cup buffalo sauce (store-bought or homemade)
- 1 cup shredded mozzarella cheese
- 1/4 cup blue cheese crumbles
- 2 green onions, sliced
- Ranch or blue cheese dressing for drizzling (optional)

Instructions:

Prepare the Pizza Dough:
- In a small bowl, combine warm water, sugar, and active dry yeast. Let it sit for 5-10 minutes until frothy.
- In a large mixing bowl, combine the flour and salt. Make a well in the center and pour in the yeast mixture and olive oil.
- Mix until the dough comes together, then knead on a floured surface for 5-7 minutes or until smooth. Place the dough in an oiled bowl, cover with a damp cloth, and let it rise for 1-2 hours until doubled in size.

Preheat the Oven:
- Preheat your oven to the highest temperature it can go (typically around 475-500°F/245-260°C). If you have a pizza stone, place it in the oven during preheating.

Roast Buffalo Cauliflower:
- Preheat the oven to 425°F (220°C).

- Toss cauliflower florets with olive oil, salt, and black pepper.
- Spread the cauliflower on a baking sheet and roast for 20-25 minutes or until golden brown and crispy.
- Remove the cauliflower from the oven and toss it in buffalo sauce until well coated.

Shape the Pizza Dough:
- Punch down the risen dough and transfer it to a floured surface. Roll it out into your desired pizza shape and thickness.

Assemble Buffalo Cauliflower Pizza:
- If using a pizza stone, transfer the rolled-out dough onto a pizza peel dusted with flour or cornmeal. If not using a stone, place the rolled-out dough on a lightly greased baking sheet.
- Spread an even layer of shredded mozzarella cheese over the dough.
- Distribute the buffalo cauliflower evenly over the cheese.
- Sprinkle blue cheese crumbles over the pizza.

Bake the Pizza:
- If using a pizza stone, carefully transfer the pizza onto the preheated stone in the oven. If not using a stone, simply place the baking sheet in the oven.
- Bake for 10-12 minutes or until the crust is golden, the cheese is melted and bubbly, and the edges are slightly crispy.

Finish and Serve:
- Remove the pizza from the oven, sprinkle sliced green onions over the top.
- Optionally, drizzle ranch or blue cheese dressing over the pizza.
- Slice and serve your mouthwatering Buffalo Cauliflower Pizza!

Enjoy the spicy kick of buffalo cauliflower combined with the creaminess of blue cheese on this unique and tasty homemade pizza. Customize it with your preferred level of heat and additional toppings if desired.

Buffalo Cauliflower Pizza

Ingredients:

Pizza Dough:

- 2 1/4 teaspoons (1 packet) active dry yeast
- 1 teaspoon sugar
- 3/4 cup warm water (110°F/43°C)
- 2 cups all-purpose flour
- 1 teaspoon salt
- 1 tablespoon olive oil

Buffalo Cauliflower Toppings:

- 3 cups cauliflower florets, cut into bite-sized pieces
- 2 tablespoons olive oil
- Salt and black pepper to taste
- 1/2 cup buffalo sauce (store-bought or homemade)
- 1 cup shredded mozzarella cheese
- 1/4 cup blue cheese crumbles
- 2 green onions, sliced
- Ranch or blue cheese dressing for drizzling (optional)

Instructions:

Prepare the Pizza Dough:
- In a small bowl, combine warm water, sugar, and active dry yeast. Let it sit for 5-10 minutes until frothy.
- In a large mixing bowl, combine the flour and salt. Make a well in the center and pour in the yeast mixture and olive oil.
- Mix until the dough comes together, then knead on a floured surface for 5-7 minutes or until smooth. Place the dough in an oiled bowl, cover with a damp cloth, and let it rise for 1-2 hours until doubled in size.

Preheat the Oven:
- Preheat your oven to the highest temperature it can go (typically around 475-500°F/245-260°C). If you have a pizza stone, place it in the oven during preheating.

Roast Buffalo Cauliflower:
- Preheat the oven to 425°F (220°C).

- Toss cauliflower florets with olive oil, salt, and black pepper.
- Spread the cauliflower on a baking sheet and roast for 20-25 minutes or until golden brown and crispy.
- Remove the cauliflower from the oven and toss it in buffalo sauce until well coated.

Shape the Pizza Dough:
- Punch down the risen dough and transfer it to a floured surface. Roll it out into your desired pizza shape and thickness.

Assemble Buffalo Cauliflower Pizza:
- If using a pizza stone, transfer the rolled-out dough onto a pizza peel dusted with flour or cornmeal. If not using a stone, place the rolled-out dough on a lightly greased baking sheet.
- Spread an even layer of shredded mozzarella cheese over the dough.
- Distribute the buffalo cauliflower evenly over the cheese.
- Sprinkle blue cheese crumbles over the pizza.

Bake the Pizza:
- If using a pizza stone, carefully transfer the pizza onto the preheated stone in the oven. If not using a stone, simply place the baking sheet in the oven.
- Bake for 10-12 minutes or until the crust is golden, the cheese is melted and bubbly, and the edges are slightly crispy.

Finish and Serve:
- Remove the pizza from the oven, sprinkle sliced green onions over the top.
- Optionally, drizzle ranch or blue cheese dressing over the pizza.
- Slice and serve your mouthwatering Buffalo Cauliflower Pizza!

Enjoy the spicy kick of buffalo cauliflower combined with the creaminess of blue cheese on this unique and tasty homemade pizza. Customize it with your preferred level of heat and additional toppings if desired.

S'mores Dessert Pizza

Ingredients:

Pizza Dough:

- 2 1/4 teaspoons (1 packet) active dry yeast
- 1 teaspoon sugar
- 3/4 cup warm water (110°F/43°C)
- 2 cups all-purpose flour
- 1 teaspoon salt
- 1 tablespoon olive oil

S'mores Toppings:

- 1 cup chocolate spread or chocolate ganache
- 1 cup mini marshmallows
- 1/2 cup graham cracker crumbs
- 1/4 cup milk chocolate chips
- 1/4 cup white chocolate chips
- 2 tablespoons chopped nuts (optional)
- 1 tablespoon powdered sugar (for dusting)
- Vanilla ice cream for serving (optional)

Instructions:

Prepare the Pizza Dough:
- In a small bowl, combine warm water, sugar, and active dry yeast. Let it sit for 5-10 minutes until frothy.
- In a large mixing bowl, combine the flour and salt. Make a well in the center and pour in the yeast mixture and olive oil.
- Mix until the dough comes together, then knead on a floured surface for 5-7 minutes or until smooth. Place the dough in an oiled bowl, cover with a damp cloth, and let it rise for 1-2 hours until doubled in size.

Preheat the Oven:
- Preheat your oven to the highest temperature it can go (typically around 475-500°F/245-260°C). If you have a pizza stone, place it in the oven during preheating.

Shape the Pizza Dough:

- Punch down the risen dough and transfer it to a floured surface. Roll it out into your desired pizza shape and thickness.

Assemble S'mores Dessert Pizza:
- If using a pizza stone, transfer the rolled-out dough onto a pizza peel dusted with flour or cornmeal. If not using a stone, place the rolled-out dough on a lightly greased baking sheet.
- Spread an even layer of chocolate spread or chocolate ganache over the dough, leaving a small border around the edges.
- Sprinkle graham cracker crumbs evenly over the chocolate.
- Distribute mini marshmallows, milk chocolate chips, and white chocolate chips over the pizza.
- Optionally, sprinkle chopped nuts over the toppings.

Bake the Pizza:
- If using a pizza stone, carefully transfer the pizza onto the preheated stone in the oven. If not using a stone, simply place the baking sheet in the oven.
- Bake for 10-12 minutes or until the crust is golden, the chocolate is melted, and the marshmallows are toasted.

Finish and Serve:
- Remove the pizza from the oven, let it cool for a few minutes, then sprinkle powdered sugar over the top.
- Optionally, serve with a scoop of vanilla ice cream.

Slice and serve your indulgent S'mores Dessert Pizza, capturing the nostalgic flavors of a classic s'mores experience in a delightful pizza form. Enjoy the gooey marshmallows, rich chocolate, and crunchy graham cracker goodness!

Caramel Apple Dessert Pizza

Ingredients:

Pizza Dough:

- 2 1/4 teaspoons (1 packet) active dry yeast
- 1 teaspoon sugar
- 3/4 cup warm water (110°F/43°C)
- 2 cups all-purpose flour
- 1 teaspoon salt
- 1 tablespoon olive oil

Caramel Apple Toppings:

- 4-5 medium-sized apples, peeled, cored, and thinly sliced
- 1/2 cup unsalted butter
- 1 cup brown sugar
- 1/4 cup heavy cream
- 1 teaspoon vanilla extract
- 1/2 teaspoon ground cinnamon
- 1/4 teaspoon salt

Streusel Topping:

- 1/2 cup all-purpose flour
- 1/4 cup brown sugar
- 1/4 cup rolled oats
- 1/4 cup unsalted butter, softened

Caramel Drizzle:

- 1/2 cup caramel sauce (store-bought or homemade)

Instructions:

Prepare the Pizza Dough:
- In a small bowl, combine warm water, sugar, and active dry yeast. Let it sit for 5-10 minutes until frothy.

- In a large mixing bowl, combine the flour and salt. Make a well in the center and pour in the yeast mixture and olive oil.
- Mix until the dough comes together, then knead on a floured surface for 5-7 minutes or until smooth. Place the dough in an oiled bowl, cover with a damp cloth, and let it rise for 1-2 hours until doubled in size.

Preheat the Oven:
- Preheat your oven to the highest temperature it can go (typically around 475-500°F/245-260°C). If you have a pizza stone, place it in the oven during preheating.

Prepare Caramel Apple Toppings:
- In a large skillet, melt butter over medium heat. Add brown sugar, heavy cream, vanilla extract, ground cinnamon, and salt. Stir until the sugar is dissolved.
- Add the sliced apples to the caramel sauce and cook for 5-7 minutes, or until the apples are softened but still have a slight bite. Set aside.

Prepare Streusel Topping:
- In a small bowl, combine flour, brown sugar, rolled oats, and softened butter. Mix until crumbly.

Shape the Pizza Dough:
- Punch down the risen dough and transfer it to a floured surface. Roll it out into your desired pizza shape and thickness.

Assemble Caramel Apple Dessert Pizza:
- If using a pizza stone, transfer the rolled-out dough onto a pizza peel dusted with flour or cornmeal. If not using a stone, place the rolled-out dough on a lightly greased baking sheet.
- Spread the caramel-coated apple slices evenly over the pizza dough.
- Sprinkle the streusel topping over the apples.

Bake the Pizza:
- If using a pizza stone, carefully transfer the pizza onto the preheated stone in the oven. If not using a stone, simply place the baking sheet in the oven.
- Bake for 12-15 minutes or until the crust is golden, and the streusel is lightly browned.

Finish and Serve:
- Remove the pizza from the oven and let it cool slightly.
- Drizzle caramel sauce over the top.
- Slice and serve your delectable Caramel Apple Dessert Pizza!

Enjoy the sweet and gooey goodness of caramel-coated apples on a dessert pizza crust, complemented by a crunchy streusel topping. It's a perfect treat for fall or any time you're craving a delicious dessert.

Chicken Pesto Flatbread

Ingredients:

Flatbread:

- 2 large flatbreads (store-bought or homemade)
- Olive oil for brushing

Pesto Sauce:

- 2 cups fresh basil leaves, packed
- 1/2 cup grated Parmesan cheese
- 1/2 cup pine nuts or walnuts
- 2 garlic cloves, peeled
- 1/2 cup extra-virgin olive oil
- Salt and black pepper to taste

Chicken Toppings:

- 1 cup cooked chicken breast, shredded or diced
- 1 cup cherry tomatoes, halved
- 1/2 cup red onion, thinly sliced
- 1 cup mozzarella cheese, shredded
- Balsamic glaze for drizzling (optional)
- Fresh basil leaves for garnish

Instructions:

Prepare Pesto Sauce:
- In a food processor, combine fresh basil, grated Parmesan cheese, pine nuts (or walnuts), and garlic cloves. Pulse until ingredients are finely chopped.
- With the food processor running, slowly pour in the olive oil until the mixture forms a smooth paste.
- Season with salt and black pepper to taste. Set aside.

Preheat the Oven:

- Preheat your oven to 400°F (200°C).

Assemble Chicken Pesto Flatbread:
- Place the flatbreads on a baking sheet.
- Brush the flatbreads with a thin layer of olive oil to prevent them from becoming too crisp.
- Spread a generous layer of pesto sauce evenly over each flatbread.

Add Chicken and Toppings:
- Distribute the cooked chicken evenly over the pesto-covered flatbreads.
- Scatter cherry tomatoes and thinly sliced red onions on top.
- Sprinkle shredded mozzarella cheese over the toppings.

Bake in the Oven:
- Bake in the preheated oven for 10-12 minutes or until the edges of the flatbread are golden, and the cheese is melted and bubbly.

Finish and Serve:
- Remove the flatbreads from the oven and let them cool for a few minutes.
- Drizzle with balsamic glaze, if desired.
- Garnish with fresh basil leaves.
- Slice and serve your delicious Chicken Pesto Flatbread!

Enjoy the delightful combination of pesto, chicken, and fresh toppings on a crispy flatbread. This dish is perfect for a quick and tasty weeknight dinner or as an appetizer for gatherings.

Margherita Naan Pizza

Ingredients:

Naan Pizza Base:

- 4 pieces of naan bread (store-bought or homemade)
- Olive oil for brushing

Margherita Toppings:

- 1 cup tomato sauce or marinara sauce
- 2 cups fresh mozzarella cheese, sliced
- 1 cup cherry tomatoes, halved
- Fresh basil leaves, torn
- Salt and black pepper to taste
- Optional: Grated Parmesan cheese

Instructions:

Preheat the Oven:
- Preheat your oven to 400°F (200°C).

Prepare Naan Pizza Base:
- Place the naan bread on a baking sheet.
- Brush each naan with a thin layer of olive oil.

Assemble Margherita Naan Pizza:
- Spread a layer of tomato sauce or marinara sauce over each naan, leaving a small border around the edges.
- Arrange slices of fresh mozzarella evenly over the sauce.
- Place halved cherry tomatoes on top of the cheese.
- Season with salt and black pepper to taste.

Bake in the Oven:
- Place the baking sheet in the preheated oven and bake for 10-12 minutes or until the cheese is melted, bubbly, and slightly golden, and the edges of the naan are crisp.

Finish and Serve:
- Remove the Margherita Naan Pizzas from the oven.
- Sprinkle torn fresh basil leaves over the top.
- Optionally, add a sprinkle of grated Parmesan cheese.

- Slice and serve immediately.

Enjoy the delicious simplicity of Margherita Naan Pizza with its combination of fresh mozzarella, juicy tomatoes, and aromatic basil. This recipe makes for a quick and satisfying meal or snack, and it's perfect for those moments when you're craving homemade pizza without the fuss of making pizza dough.

Roasted Veggie Naan Pizza

Ingredients:

Naan Pizza Base:

- 4 pieces of naan bread (store-bought or homemade)
- Olive oil for brushing

Roasted Veggie Toppings:

- 1 zucchini, thinly sliced
- 1 bell pepper, thinly sliced
- 1 red onion, thinly sliced
- 1 cup cherry tomatoes, halved
- 2 tablespoons olive oil
- 1 teaspoon dried oregano
- Salt and black pepper to taste

Cheese (Optional):

- 1 cup shredded mozzarella cheese
- 1/4 cup grated Parmesan cheese

Additional Toppings (Optional):

- Fresh basil leaves, torn
- Red pepper flakes
- Balsamic glaze

Instructions:

Preheat the Oven:
- Preheat your oven to 400°F (200°C).

Prepare Naan Pizza Base:
- Place the naan bread on a baking sheet.
- Brush each naan with a thin layer of olive oil.

Prepare Roasted Veggie Toppings:

- In a bowl, toss the sliced zucchini, bell pepper, red onion, and cherry tomatoes with olive oil, dried oregano, salt, and black pepper until well coated.
- Spread the seasoned veggies on a separate baking sheet in a single layer.

Roast the Veggies:
- Place the baking sheet with the veggies in the preheated oven.
- Roast for 15-20 minutes or until the vegetables are tender and slightly caramelized.

Assemble Roasted Veggie Naan Pizza:
- Spread the roasted veggies evenly over each naan bread, leaving a small border around the edges.
- If desired, sprinkle shredded mozzarella cheese and grated Parmesan cheese over the veggies.

Bake in the Oven:
- Place the baking sheet with the assembled pizzas in the preheated oven.
- Bake for 10-12 minutes or until the cheese is melted and bubbly, and the edges of the naan are crisp.

Finish and Serve:
- Remove the Roasted Veggie Naan Pizzas from the oven.
- If desired, sprinkle torn fresh basil leaves, red pepper flakes, and drizzle with balsamic glaze.
- Slice and serve immediately.

Enjoy the delightful combination of roasted vegetables on a naan bread crust. This recipe allows for customization, so feel free to add your favorite cheeses or additional toppings to suit your taste. It's a quick and delicious way to enjoy a veggie-packed pizza!

Prosciutto and Arugula Flatbread

Ingredients:

Flatbread:

- 4 pieces of flatbread (store-bought or homemade)
- Olive oil for brushing

Prosciutto and Arugula Toppings:

- 8 slices of prosciutto
- 2 cups arugula, washed and dried
- 1 cup cherry tomatoes, halved
- 1/2 cup shaved Parmesan cheese
- Balsamic glaze for drizzling
- Salt and black pepper to taste

Instructions:

Preheat the Oven:
- Preheat your oven to 400°F (200°C).

Prepare Flatbread:
- Place the flatbreads on a baking sheet.
- Brush each flatbread with a thin layer of olive oil.

Assemble Prosciutto and Arugula Flatbread:
- Lay out slices of prosciutto evenly over each flatbread.
- Scatter halved cherry tomatoes on top of the prosciutto.
- If desired, sprinkle salt and black pepper over the toppings.

Bake in the Oven:
- Place the baking sheet with the assembled flatbreads in the preheated oven.
- Bake for 8-10 minutes or until the edges of the flatbread are golden, and the prosciutto is slightly crispy.

Finish and Serve:
- Remove the flatbreads from the oven.
- Evenly distribute arugula over the flatbreads.
- Sprinkle shaved Parmesan cheese over the top.
- Drizzle with balsamic glaze for added flavor.

- Slice and serve your Prosciutto and Arugula Flatbreads immediately.

Enjoy the delightful contrast of the salty prosciutto, peppery arugula, and the sweetness of balsamic glaze on a crispy flatbread. This recipe is quick to prepare and makes for a flavorful appetizer or light meal.

Fig and Goat Cheese Flatbread

Ingredients:

Flatbread:

- 4 pieces of flatbread (store-bought or homemade)
- Olive oil for brushing

Fig and Goat Cheese Toppings:

- 1 cup fig preserves or fresh figs, sliced
- 1 cup goat cheese, crumbled
- 1/2 cup caramelized onions
- 1/4 cup chopped walnuts or pecans
- Fresh thyme leaves for garnish
- Honey for drizzling
- Salt and black pepper to taste

Instructions:

Preheat the Oven:
- Preheat your oven to 400°F (200°C).

Prepare Flatbread:
- Place the flatbreads on a baking sheet.
- Brush each flatbread with a thin layer of olive oil.

Assemble Fig and Goat Cheese Flatbread:
- Spread a layer of fig preserves or arrange sliced fresh figs evenly over each flatbread.
- Sprinkle crumbled goat cheese over the figs.
- Distribute caramelized onions on top of the goat cheese.
- If desired, sprinkle chopped walnuts or pecans over the toppings.
- Season with salt and black pepper to taste.

Bake in the Oven:
- Place the baking sheet with the assembled flatbreads in the preheated oven.
- Bake for 8-10 minutes or until the edges of the flatbread are golden, and the goat cheese is slightly melted.

Finish and Serve:
- Remove the flatbreads from the oven.
- Garnish with fresh thyme leaves.

- Drizzle honey over the top.
- Slice and serve your Fig and Goat Cheese Flatbreads immediately.

Enjoy the wonderful combination of sweet figs, tangy goat cheese, and the richness of caramelized onions on a crispy flatbread. This recipe is perfect for a sophisticated appetizer or a light and flavorful meal.

Ratatouille Pizza

Ingredients:

Pizza Dough:

- 2 1/4 teaspoons (1 packet) active dry yeast
- 1 teaspoon sugar
- 3/4 cup warm water (110°F/43°C)
- 2 cups all-purpose flour
- 1 teaspoon salt
- 1 tablespoon olive oil

Ratatouille Toppings:

- 1 small eggplant, thinly sliced
- 1 small zucchini, thinly sliced
- 1 small yellow squash, thinly sliced
- 1 bell pepper, thinly sliced
- 1 small red onion, thinly sliced
- 2 tablespoons olive oil
- 2 cloves garlic, minced
- 1 teaspoon dried thyme
- 1 teaspoon dried oregano
- Salt and black pepper to taste

Other Toppings:

- 1 cup shredded mozzarella cheese
- 1/4 cup grated Parmesan cheese
- Fresh basil leaves for garnish

Instructions:

Prepare Pizza Dough:
- In a small bowl, combine warm water, sugar, and active dry yeast. Let it sit for 5-10 minutes until frothy.
- In a large mixing bowl, combine the flour and salt. Make a well in the center and pour in the yeast mixture and olive oil.

- Mix until the dough comes together, then knead on a floured surface for 5-7 minutes or until smooth. Place the dough in an oiled bowl, cover with a damp cloth, and let it rise for 1-2 hours until doubled in size.

Preheat the Oven:
- Preheat your oven to the highest temperature it can go (typically around 475-500°F/245-260°C). If you have a pizza stone, place it in the oven during preheating.

Prepare Ratatouille Toppings:
- In a large skillet, heat olive oil over medium heat. Add minced garlic and cook for 1 minute until fragrant.
- Add the sliced eggplant, zucchini, yellow squash, bell pepper, and red onion to the skillet.
- Sprinkle dried thyme, dried oregano, salt, and black pepper over the vegetables. Sauté for 8-10 minutes or until the vegetables are tender but still hold their shape. Set aside.

Shape the Pizza Dough:
- Punch down the risen dough and transfer it to a floured surface. Roll it out into your desired pizza shape and thickness.

Assemble Ratatouille Pizza:
- If using a pizza stone, transfer the rolled-out dough onto a pizza peel dusted with flour or cornmeal. If not using a stone, place the rolled-out dough on a lightly greased baking sheet.
- Spread an even layer of shredded mozzarella cheese over the dough.
- Distribute the sautéed ratatouille vegetables evenly over the cheese.
- Sprinkle grated Parmesan cheese over the toppings.

Bake the Pizza:
- If using a pizza stone, carefully transfer the pizza onto the preheated stone in the oven. If not using a stone, simply place the baking sheet in the oven.
- Bake for 10-12 minutes or until the crust is golden, the cheese is melted and bubbly, and the edges are slightly crispy.

Finish and Serve:
- Remove the pizza from the oven, sprinkle fresh basil leaves over the top.
- Slice and serve your Ratatouille Pizza, capturing the essence of the French classic in a delightful pizza form.

Enjoy the rustic and hearty flavors of ratatouille on a crispy pizza crust. This recipe brings a touch of elegance to pizza night with its colorful and savory vegetable topping.

Mediterranean Flatbread

Ingredients:

Flatbread:

- 4 pieces of flatbread (store-bought or homemade)
- Olive oil for brushing

Hummus Spread:

- 1 cup hummus (store-bought or homemade)

Mediterranean Toppings:

- 1 cup cherry tomatoes, halved
- 1 cucumber, thinly sliced
- 1/2 cup Kalamata olives, sliced
- 1/2 cup feta cheese, crumbled
- 1/4 cup red onion, thinly sliced
- Fresh parsley, chopped
- Lemon wedges for serving

Optional Additions:

- Roasted red peppers
- Artichoke hearts
- Pepperoncini

Instructions:

Preheat the Oven:
- Preheat your oven to 400°F (200°C).

Prepare Flatbread:
- Place the flatbreads on a baking sheet.
- Brush each flatbread with a thin layer of olive oil.

Assemble Mediterranean Flatbread:
- Spread a generous layer of hummus over each flatbread, leaving a small border around the edges.

- Arrange halved cherry tomatoes, sliced cucumber, Kalamata olives, crumbled feta cheese, and thinly sliced red onion on top of the hummus.
- Add any optional ingredients like roasted red peppers, artichoke hearts, or pepperoncini if desired.

Bake in the Oven:
- Place the baking sheet with the assembled flatbreads in the preheated oven.
- Bake for 8-10 minutes or until the edges of the flatbread are golden, and the toppings are heated through.

Finish and Serve:
- Remove the Mediterranean Flatbreads from the oven.
- Sprinkle fresh chopped parsley over the top.
- Serve with lemon wedges on the side.

Enjoy the vibrant and fresh flavors of the Mediterranean with this flatbread. It's a versatile dish, and you can customize it with your favorite Mediterranean ingredients. This makes for a fantastic appetizer, light lunch, or even a shareable snack during gatherings.

BBQ Pulled Pork Pizza

Ingredients:

Pizza Dough:

- 2 1/4 teaspoons (1 packet) active dry yeast
- 1 teaspoon sugar
- 3/4 cup warm water (110°F/43°C)
- 2 cups all-purpose flour
- 1 teaspoon salt
- 1 tablespoon olive oil

BBQ Pulled Pork:

- 2 cups cooked and shredded pulled pork
- 1 cup barbecue sauce (store-bought or homemade)

Pizza Toppings:

- 1 cup shredded mozzarella cheese
- 1/2 red onion, thinly sliced
- 1/2 cup sliced bell peppers (red, green, or a mix)
- 1/4 cup chopped fresh cilantro
- 1/4 cup sliced jalapeños (optional for heat)
- Cornmeal or flour for dusting

Instructions:

Prepare Pizza Dough:
- In a small bowl, combine warm water, sugar, and active dry yeast. Let it sit for 5-10 minutes until frothy.
- In a large mixing bowl, combine the flour and salt. Make a well in the center and pour in the yeast mixture and olive oil.
- Mix until the dough comes together, then knead on a floured surface for 5-7 minutes or until smooth. Place the dough in an oiled bowl, cover with a damp cloth, and let it rise for 1-2 hours until doubled in size.

Preheat the Oven:

- Preheat your oven to the highest temperature it can go (typically around 475-500°F/245-260°C). If you have a pizza stone, place it in the oven during preheating.

Prepare BBQ Pulled Pork:
- In a bowl, mix the shredded pulled pork with the barbecue sauce until well coated. Set aside.

Shape the Pizza Dough:
- Punch down the risen dough and transfer it to a floured surface. Roll it out into your desired pizza shape and thickness.

Assemble BBQ Pulled Pork Pizza:
- If using a pizza stone, transfer the rolled-out dough onto a pizza peel dusted with flour or cornmeal. If not using a stone, place the rolled-out dough on a lightly greased baking sheet.
- Spread an even layer of shredded mozzarella cheese over the dough.
- Distribute the BBQ pulled pork evenly over the cheese.
- Scatter sliced red onion, bell peppers, and jalapeños (if using) over the pizza.

Bake the Pizza:
- If using a pizza stone, carefully transfer the pizza onto the preheated stone in the oven. If not using a stone, simply place the baking sheet in the oven.
- Bake for 10-12 minutes or until the crust is golden, the cheese is melted and bubbly, and the edges are slightly crispy.

Finish and Serve:
- Remove the pizza from the oven, sprinkle chopped fresh cilantro over the top.
- Slice and serve your mouthwatering BBQ Pulled Pork Pizza!

Enjoy the smoky, savory flavors of BBQ pulled pork on a crispy pizza crust. This recipe is perfect for a hearty and satisfying meal, and it's sure to be a hit with BBQ lovers.

Bruschetta Pizza

Ingredients:

Pizza Dough:

- 2 1/4 teaspoons (1 packet) active dry yeast
- 1 teaspoon sugar
- 3/4 cup warm water (110°F/43°C)
- 2 cups all-purpose flour
- 1 teaspoon salt
- 1 tablespoon olive oil

Bruschetta Topping:

- 4 medium tomatoes, diced
- 1/2 cup fresh basil, chopped
- 3 cloves garlic, minced
- 2 tablespoons balsamic vinegar
- 2 tablespoons extra-virgin olive oil
- Salt and black pepper to taste

Pizza Toppings:

- 1 cup shredded mozzarella cheese
- 1/4 cup grated Parmesan cheese
- Balsamic glaze for drizzling (optional)

Instructions:

Prepare Pizza Dough:
- In a small bowl, combine warm water, sugar, and active dry yeast. Let it sit for 5-10 minutes until frothy.
- In a large mixing bowl, combine the flour and salt. Make a well in the center and pour in the yeast mixture and olive oil.
- Mix until the dough comes together, then knead on a floured surface for 5-7 minutes or until smooth. Place the dough in an oiled bowl, cover with a damp cloth, and let it rise for 1-2 hours until doubled in size.

Preheat the Oven:

- Preheat your oven to the highest temperature it can go (typically around 475-500°F/245-260°C). If you have a pizza stone, place it in the oven during preheating.

Prepare Bruschetta Topping:
- In a bowl, combine diced tomatoes, chopped fresh basil, minced garlic, balsamic vinegar, extra-virgin olive oil, salt, and black pepper. Mix well and set aside.

Shape the Pizza Dough:
- Punch down the risen dough and transfer it to a floured surface. Roll it out into your desired pizza shape and thickness.

Assemble Bruschetta Pizza:
- If using a pizza stone, transfer the rolled-out dough onto a pizza peel dusted with flour or cornmeal. If not using a stone, place the rolled-out dough on a lightly greased baking sheet.
- Spread an even layer of shredded mozzarella cheese over the dough.
- Spoon the prepared bruschetta topping evenly over the cheese.
- Sprinkle grated Parmesan cheese over the toppings.

Bake the Pizza:
- If using a pizza stone, carefully transfer the pizza onto the preheated stone in the oven. If not using a stone, simply place the baking sheet in the oven.
- Bake for 10-12 minutes or until the crust is golden, the cheese is melted and bubbly, and the edges are slightly crispy.

Finish and Serve:
- Remove the pizza from the oven.
- Optionally, drizzle with balsamic glaze for added flavor.
- Slice and serve your delectable Bruschetta Pizza!

Enjoy the fresh and vibrant flavors of bruschetta on a crispy pizza crust. This recipe is perfect for a light and flavorful meal, and it's a great way to showcase the delicious simplicity of classic Italian ingredients.

Pear and Gorgonzola Pizza

Ingredients:

Pizza Dough:

- 2 1/4 teaspoons (1 packet) active dry yeast
- 1 teaspoon sugar
- 3/4 cup warm water (110°F/43°C)
- 2 cups all-purpose flour
- 1 teaspoon salt
- 1 tablespoon olive oil

Pizza Toppings:

- 2 ripe pears, thinly sliced
- 1 cup Gorgonzola cheese, crumbled
- 1/2 cup chopped walnuts or pecans
- 1/4 cup honey
- 2 tablespoons balsamic glaze (optional)
- Fresh arugula for garnish (optional)

Instructions:

Prepare Pizza Dough:
- In a small bowl, combine warm water, sugar, and active dry yeast. Let it sit for 5-10 minutes until frothy.
- In a large mixing bowl, combine the flour and salt. Make a well in the center and pour in the yeast mixture and olive oil.
- Mix until the dough comes together, then knead on a floured surface for 5-7 minutes or until smooth. Place the dough in an oiled bowl, cover with a damp cloth, and let it rise for 1-2 hours until doubled in size.

Preheat the Oven:
- Preheat your oven to the highest temperature it can go (typically around 475-500°F/245-260°C). If you have a pizza stone, place it in the oven during preheating.

Shape the Pizza Dough:
- Punch down the risen dough and transfer it to a floured surface. Roll it out into your desired pizza shape and thickness.

Assemble Pear and Gorgonzola Pizza:
- If using a pizza stone, transfer the rolled-out dough onto a pizza peel dusted with flour or cornmeal. If not using a stone, place the rolled-out dough on a lightly greased baking sheet.
- Arrange the thinly sliced pears evenly over the pizza dough.
- Sprinkle crumbled Gorgonzola cheese and chopped walnuts or pecans over the pears.

Bake the Pizza:
- If using a pizza stone, carefully transfer the pizza onto the preheated stone in the oven. If not using a stone, simply place the baking sheet in the oven.
- Bake for 10-12 minutes or until the crust is golden, the cheese is melted and bubbly, and the edges are slightly crispy.

Finish and Serve:
- Remove the pizza from the oven.
- Drizzle honey over the top.
- Optionally, drizzle balsamic glaze for added depth of flavor.
- Garnish with fresh arugula if desired.
- Slice and serve your delicious Pear and Gorgonzola Pizza!

Enjoy the perfect balance of sweet and savory with the juicy pears, creamy Gorgonzola, and the crunch of nuts on a crispy pizza crust. This pizza is an elegant and tasty choice for a unique and gourmet homemade pizza experience.

Buffalo Ranch Chicken Pizza

Ingredients:

Pizza Dough:

- 2 1/4 teaspoons (1 packet) active dry yeast
- 1 teaspoon sugar
- 3/4 cup warm water (110°F/43°C)
- 2 cups all-purpose flour
- 1 teaspoon salt
- 1 tablespoon olive oil

Buffalo Ranch Chicken:

- 1 cup cooked and shredded chicken
- 1/2 cup buffalo sauce
- 2 tablespoons ranch dressing
- 1 tablespoon melted butter
- 1 clove garlic, minced

Pizza Toppings:

- 1 cup shredded mozzarella cheese
- 1/4 cup blue cheese crumbles
- 2 green onions, thinly sliced
- Fresh cilantro or parsley for garnish

Instructions:

   Prepare Pizza Dough:
   - In a small bowl, combine warm water, sugar, and active dry yeast. Let it sit for 5-10 minutes until frothy.
   - In a large mixing bowl, combine the flour and salt. Make a well in the center and pour in the yeast mixture and olive oil.

- Mix until the dough comes together, then knead on a floured surface for 5-7 minutes or until smooth. Place the dough in an oiled bowl, cover with a damp cloth, and let it rise for 1-2 hours until doubled in size.

Preheat the Oven:
- Preheat your oven to the highest temperature it can go (typically around 475-500°F/245-260°C). If you have a pizza stone, place it in the oven during preheating.

Prepare Buffalo Ranch Chicken:
- In a bowl, combine shredded chicken with buffalo sauce, ranch dressing, melted butter, and minced garlic. Mix until well coated.

Shape the Pizza Dough:
- Punch down the risen dough and transfer it to a floured surface. Roll it out into your desired pizza shape and thickness.

Assemble Buffalo Ranch Chicken Pizza:
- If using a pizza stone, transfer the rolled-out dough onto a pizza peel dusted with flour or cornmeal. If not using a stone, place the rolled-out dough on a lightly greased baking sheet.
- Spread an even layer of shredded mozzarella cheese over the dough.
- Spoon the buffalo ranch chicken mixture evenly over the cheese.
- Sprinkle blue cheese crumbles over the chicken.
- If desired, add sliced green onions on top.

Bake the Pizza:
- If using a pizza stone, carefully transfer the pizza onto the preheated stone in the oven. If not using a stone, simply place the baking sheet in the oven.
- Bake for 10-12 minutes or until the crust is golden, the cheese is melted and bubbly, and the edges are slightly crispy.

Finish and Serve:
- Remove the pizza from the oven.
- Garnish with fresh cilantro or parsley.
- Slice and serve your zesty Buffalo Ranch Chicken Pizza!

Enjoy the bold flavors of buffalo sauce and ranch dressing combined with tender chicken on a crispy pizza crust. This pizza is perfect for those who love a bit of heat and a cool, creamy kick.

Asparagus and Parmesan Pizza

Ingredients:

Pizza Dough:

- 2 1/4 teaspoons (1 packet) active dry yeast
- 1 teaspoon sugar
- 3/4 cup warm water (110°F/43°C)
- 2 cups all-purpose flour
- 1 teaspoon salt
- 1 tablespoon olive oil

Pizza Toppings:

- 1 bunch asparagus, trimmed and cut into 2-inch pieces
- 2 tablespoons olive oil
- Salt and black pepper to taste
- 1 cup shredded mozzarella cheese
- 1/2 cup grated Parmesan cheese
- 2 cloves garlic, minced
- Zest of 1 lemon
- Red pepper flakes (optional)
- Fresh basil leaves for garnish

Instructions:

Prepare Pizza Dough:
- In a small bowl, combine warm water, sugar, and active dry yeast. Let it sit for 5-10 minutes until frothy.
- In a large mixing bowl, combine the flour and salt. Make a well in the center and pour in the yeast mixture and olive oil.
- Mix until the dough comes together, then knead on a floured surface for 5-7 minutes or until smooth. Place the dough in an oiled bowl, cover with a damp cloth, and let it rise for 1-2 hours until doubled in size.

Preheat the Oven:
- Preheat your oven to the highest temperature it can go (typically around 475-500°F/245-260°C). If you have a pizza stone, place it in the oven during preheating.

Prepare Asparagus:
- In a bowl, toss asparagus pieces with olive oil, salt, and black pepper.

Shape the Pizza Dough:
- Punch down the risen dough and transfer it to a floured surface. Roll it out into your desired pizza shape and thickness.

Assemble Asparagus and Parmesan Pizza:
- If using a pizza stone, transfer the rolled-out dough onto a pizza peel dusted with flour or cornmeal. If not using a stone, place the rolled-out dough on a lightly greased baking sheet.
- Spread an even layer of shredded mozzarella cheese over the dough.
- Arrange the asparagus pieces evenly on top of the cheese.
- Sprinkle grated Parmesan cheese over the asparagus.
- Scatter minced garlic and lemon zest over the toppings.
- If desired, add a pinch of red pepper flakes for some heat.

Bake the Pizza:
- If using a pizza stone, carefully transfer the pizza onto the preheated stone in the oven. If not using a stone, simply place the baking sheet in the oven.
- Bake for 10-12 minutes or until the crust is golden, the cheese is melted and bubbly, and the edges are slightly crispy.

Finish and Serve:
- Remove the pizza from the oven.
- Garnish with fresh basil leaves.
- Slice and serve your delightful Asparagus and Parmesan Pizza!

Enjoy the light and fresh flavors of asparagus paired with the nuttiness of Parmesan on a crispy pizza crust. This pizza is a wonderful way to showcase the seasonal goodness of asparagus in a simple and delicious meal.

Quattro Formaggi Pizza

Ingredients:

Pizza Dough:

- 2 1/4 teaspoons (1 packet) active dry yeast
- 1 teaspoon sugar
- 3/4 cup warm water (110°F/43°C)
- 2 cups all-purpose flour
- 1 teaspoon salt
- 1 tablespoon olive oil

Four Cheese Blend:

- 1 cup shredded mozzarella cheese
- 1/2 cup Gorgonzola cheese, crumbled
- 1/2 cup Fontina cheese, shredded
- 1/2 cup Parmesan cheese, grated
- 1/4 cup fresh basil, chopped
- 2 tablespoons olive oil (for drizzling)

Instructions:

Prepare Pizza Dough:
- In a small bowl, combine warm water, sugar, and active dry yeast. Let it sit for 5-10 minutes until frothy.
- In a large mixing bowl, combine the flour and salt. Make a well in the center and pour in the yeast mixture and olive oil.
- Mix until the dough comes together, then knead on a floured surface for 5-7 minutes or until smooth. Place the dough in an oiled bowl, cover with a damp cloth, and let it rise for 1-2 hours until doubled in size.

Preheat the Oven:
- Preheat your oven to the highest temperature it can go (typically around 475-500°F/245-260°C). If you have a pizza stone, place it in the oven during preheating.

Shape the Pizza Dough:
- Punch down the risen dough and transfer it to a floured surface. Roll it out into your desired pizza shape and thickness.

Prepare Four Cheese Blend:
- In a bowl, combine shredded mozzarella, crumbled Gorgonzola, shredded Fontina, and grated Parmesan. Mix well to create the four cheese blend.

Assemble Quattro Formaggi Pizza:
- If using a pizza stone, transfer the rolled-out dough onto a pizza peel dusted with flour or cornmeal. If not using a stone, place the rolled-out dough on a lightly greased baking sheet.
- Spread an even layer of the four cheese blend over the dough.
- Sprinkle chopped fresh basil over the cheese.
- Drizzle olive oil over the top.

Bake the Pizza:
- If using a pizza stone, carefully transfer the pizza onto the preheated stone in the oven. If not using a stone, simply place the baking sheet in the oven.
- Bake for 10-12 minutes or until the crust is golden, the cheese is melted and bubbly, and the edges are slightly crispy.

Finish and Serve:
- Remove the pizza from the oven.
- Slice and serve your indulgent Quattro Formaggi Pizza immediately.

Enjoy the luxurious combination of four different cheeses on a crispy pizza crust. This pizza is a cheese lover's delight, and the blend of mozzarella, Gorgonzola, Fontina, and Parmesan creates a harmonious and delicious flavor profile.

Philly Cheesesteak Flatbread

Ingredients:

Flatbread:

- 4 pieces of flatbread (store-bought or homemade)

Philly Cheesesteak Toppings:

- 1 pound thinly sliced beef sirloin or ribeye
- 1 large onion, thinly sliced
- 1 bell pepper (green or red), thinly sliced
- 2 tablespoons olive oil
- Salt and black pepper to taste
- 1 teaspoon Worcestershire sauce
- 1 cup shredded provolone cheese (or a blend of provolone and American cheese)
- Fresh parsley, chopped for garnish (optional)

Garlic Aioli:

- 1/2 cup mayonnaise
- 1 clove garlic, minced
- 1 tablespoon fresh lemon juice
- Salt and black pepper to taste

Instructions:

Prepare Flatbread:
- If using store-bought flatbread, follow the package instructions for pre-baking or heating. If making homemade flatbread, prepare and bake according to the recipe.

Prepare Philly Cheesesteak Toppings:
- In a large skillet, heat olive oil over medium-high heat.
- Add thinly sliced beef to the skillet and cook until browned. Season with salt and black pepper.
- Add sliced onions and bell peppers to the skillet and cook until softened.

- Stir in Worcestershire sauce and continue cooking until the beef is cooked through and the vegetables are tender.

Prepare Garlic Aioli:
- In a small bowl, combine mayonnaise, minced garlic, fresh lemon juice, salt, and black pepper. Mix well to create the garlic aioli.

Assemble Philly Cheesesteak Flatbread:
- Spread a layer of the cooked Philly Cheesesteak mixture evenly over each flatbread.
- Sprinkle shredded provolone cheese (or the cheese blend) over the toppings.

Bake or Broil:
- Preheat your oven's broiler or bake the flatbreads in the oven according to the flatbread package instructions.
- If broiling, place the flatbreads under the broiler for a few minutes until the cheese is melted and bubbly, and the edges are slightly crispy.

Finish and Serve:
- Remove the flatbreads from the oven.
- Drizzle garlic aioli over the top.
- Garnish with chopped fresh parsley if desired.

Slice and Enjoy:
- Slice the Philly Cheesesteak Flatbreads into portions and serve immediately.

Enjoy the savory and cheesy goodness of a Philly Cheesesteak in a convenient flatbread format. This recipe is perfect for a quick and satisfying meal with all the flavors of the classic sandwich.

Chicken Tikka Masala Pizza

Ingredients:

Pizza Dough:

- 2 1/4 teaspoons (1 packet) active dry yeast
- 1 teaspoon sugar
- 3/4 cup warm water (110°F/43°C)
- 2 cups all-purpose flour
- 1 teaspoon salt
- 1 tablespoon olive oil

Chicken Tikka Masala:

- 1 pound boneless, skinless chicken breast, cut into bite-sized pieces
- 1 cup plain yogurt
- 2 tablespoons Tikka Masala spice blend
- 2 tablespoons vegetable oil
- 1 large onion, finely chopped
- 3 cloves garlic, minced
- 1 can (14 ounces) crushed tomatoes
- 1/2 cup heavy cream
- Salt and black pepper to taste
- Fresh cilantro, chopped for garnish

Pizza Toppings:

- 1 cup shredded mozzarella cheese
- 1/2 cup crumbled paneer (Indian cheese)
- Sliced red onion
- Sliced bell peppers (red and green)
- Fresh cilantro for garnish

Instructions:

Prepare Pizza Dough:
- In a small bowl, combine warm water, sugar, and active dry yeast. Let it sit for 5-10 minutes until frothy.

- In a large mixing bowl, combine the flour and salt. Make a well in the center and pour in the yeast mixture and olive oil.
- Mix until the dough comes together, then knead on a floured surface for 5-7 minutes or until smooth. Place the dough in an oiled bowl, cover with a damp cloth, and let it rise for 1-2 hours until doubled in size.

Prepare Chicken Tikka Masala:
- In a bowl, combine yogurt and Tikka Masala spice blend. Add the chicken pieces and marinate for at least 30 minutes.
- In a large skillet, heat vegetable oil over medium heat. Add finely chopped onion and cook until translucent.
- Add minced garlic and marinated chicken to the skillet. Cook until the chicken is browned on all sides.
- Stir in crushed tomatoes and simmer for 10-15 minutes.
- Pour in heavy cream and season with salt and black pepper. Simmer for an additional 5 minutes until the sauce thickens.
- Garnish with chopped cilantro and set aside.

Shape the Pizza Dough:
- Punch down the risen dough and transfer it to a floured surface. Roll it out into your desired pizza shape and thickness.

Assemble Chicken Tikka Masala Pizza:
- If using a pizza stone, transfer the rolled-out dough onto a pizza peel dusted with flour or cornmeal. If not using a stone, place the rolled-out dough on a lightly greased baking sheet.
- Spread an even layer of shredded mozzarella cheese over the dough.
- Spoon the prepared Chicken Tikka Masala over the cheese.
- Scatter crumbled paneer, sliced red onion, and sliced bell peppers on top.

Bake the Pizza:
- If using a pizza stone, carefully transfer the pizza onto the preheated stone in the oven. If not using a stone, simply place the baking sheet in the oven.
- Bake for 10-12 minutes or until the crust is golden, the cheese is melted and bubbly, and the edges are slightly crispy.

Finish and Serve:
- Remove the pizza from the oven.
- Garnish with fresh cilantro.
- Slice and serve your delightful Chicken Tikka Masala Pizza!

Enjoy the fusion of Indian and Italian flavors with this unique and delicious pizza. The aromatic spices of Chicken Tikka Masala paired with the cheesy goodness of pizza make for a delightful and satisfying meal.

Reuben Pizza

Ingredients:

Pizza Dough:

- 2 1/4 teaspoons (1 packet) active dry yeast
- 1 teaspoon sugar
- 3/4 cup warm water (110°F/43°C)
- 2 cups all-purpose flour
- 1 teaspoon salt
- 1 tablespoon olive oil

Reuben Pizza Toppings:

- 1/2 cup Thousand Island dressing
- 1 1/2 cups shredded Swiss cheese
- 1 cup cooked corned beef, thinly sliced or shredded
- 1 cup sauerkraut, drained
- 1/4 cup chopped fresh parsley (optional, for garnish)
- Rye bread crumbs or crushed rye crackers (optional, for added texture)

Instructions:

Prepare Pizza Dough:
- In a small bowl, combine warm water, sugar, and active dry yeast. Let it sit for 5-10 minutes until frothy.
- In a large mixing bowl, combine the flour and salt. Make a well in the center and pour in the yeast mixture and olive oil.
- Mix until the dough comes together, then knead on a floured surface for 5-7 minutes or until smooth. Place the dough in an oiled bowl, cover with a damp cloth, and let it rise for 1-2 hours until doubled in size.

Preheat the Oven:
- Preheat your oven to the highest temperature it can go (typically around 475-500°F/245-260°C). If you have a pizza stone, place it in the oven during preheating.

Shape the Pizza Dough:
- Punch down the risen dough and transfer it to a floured surface. Roll it out into your desired pizza shape and thickness.

Assemble Reuben Pizza:
- If using a pizza stone, transfer the rolled-out dough onto a pizza peel dusted with flour or cornmeal. If not using a stone, place the rolled-out dough on a lightly greased baking sheet.
- Spread an even layer of Thousand Island dressing over the dough, leaving a small border around the edges.
- Sprinkle shredded Swiss cheese evenly over the dressing.
- Distribute the cooked corned beef and sauerkraut over the cheese.

Bake the Pizza:
- If using a pizza stone, carefully transfer the pizza onto the preheated stone in the oven. If not using a stone, simply place the baking sheet in the oven.
- Bake for 10-12 minutes or until the crust is golden, the cheese is melted and bubbly, and the edges are slightly crispy.

Finish and Serve:
- Remove the pizza from the oven.
- If desired, sprinkle chopped fresh parsley and rye bread crumbs or crushed rye crackers over the top.
- Slice and serve your delicious Reuben Pizza!

Enjoy the unique and savory flavors of a Reuben sandwich in pizza form. This recipe is a fun and flavorful twist on a classic favorite, and it's perfect for pizza and sandwich lovers alike.

Caramelized Pear and Brie Pizza

Ingredients:

Pizza Dough:

- 2 1/4 teaspoons (1 packet) active dry yeast
- 1 teaspoon sugar
- 3/4 cup warm water (110°F/43°C)
- 2 cups all-purpose flour
- 1 teaspoon salt
- 1 tablespoon olive oil

Caramelized Pear Topping:

- 2 ripe but firm pears, thinly sliced
- 2 tablespoons unsalted butter
- 3 tablespoons brown sugar
- 1/4 teaspoon ground cinnamon
- Pinch of salt

Pizza Toppings:

- 8 ounces brie cheese, rind removed and sliced
- 1/2 cup chopped walnuts or pecans
- Honey for drizzling
- Fresh arugula for garnish (optional)

Instructions:

Prepare Pizza Dough:
- In a small bowl, combine warm water, sugar, and active dry yeast. Let it sit for 5-10 minutes until frothy.
- In a large mixing bowl, combine the flour and salt. Make a well in the center and pour in the yeast mixture and olive oil.
- Mix until the dough comes together, then knead on a floured surface for 5-7 minutes or until smooth. Place the dough in an oiled bowl, cover with a damp cloth, and let it rise for 1-2 hours until doubled in size.

Preheat the Oven:

- Preheat your oven to the highest temperature it can go (typically around 475-500°F/245-260°C). If you have a pizza stone, place it in the oven during preheating.

Prepare Caramelized Pear Topping:
- In a skillet, melt butter over medium heat. Add thinly sliced pears and cook for 2-3 minutes until slightly softened.
- Sprinkle brown sugar, ground cinnamon, and a pinch of salt over the pears. Stir to combine.
- Cook for an additional 5-7 minutes, stirring occasionally, until the pears are caramelized and the sugar has melted. Remove from heat and set aside.

Shape the Pizza Dough:
- Punch down the risen dough and transfer it to a floured surface. Roll it out into your desired pizza shape and thickness.

Assemble Caramelized Pear and Brie Pizza:
- If using a pizza stone, transfer the rolled-out dough onto a pizza peel dusted with flour or cornmeal. If not using a stone, place the rolled-out dough on a lightly greased baking sheet.
- Arrange slices of brie cheese over the dough.
- Spread the caramelized pear mixture evenly over the cheese.
- Sprinkle chopped walnuts or pecans over the top.

Bake the Pizza:
- If using a pizza stone, carefully transfer the pizza onto the preheated stone in the oven. If not using a stone, simply place the baking sheet in the oven.
- Bake for 10-12 minutes or until the crust is golden, the cheese is melted and bubbly, and the edges are slightly crispy.

Finish and Serve:
- Remove the pizza from the oven.
- Drizzle honey over the top.
- Optionally, garnish with fresh arugula for a peppery contrast.
- Slice and serve your elegant Caramelized Pear and Brie Pizza!

Enjoy the sweet and savory combination of caramelized pears and creamy brie on a crispy pizza crust. This pizza is perfect for a sophisticated and delicious meal, and it's sure to impress your taste buds.

Buffalo Cauliflower Flatbread

Ingredients:

Flatbread:

- 4 pieces of flatbread (store-bought or homemade)

Buffalo Cauliflower:

- 1 small head of cauliflower, cut into small florets
- 2 tablespoons olive oil
- 1/2 cup buffalo sauce
- 1 tablespoon melted butter
- 1 teaspoon garlic powder
- Salt and black pepper to taste

Flatbread Toppings:

- 1 cup shredded mozzarella cheese
- 1/4 cup crumbled blue cheese
- 2 green onions, thinly sliced
- Ranch or blue cheese dressing for drizzling

Instructions:

Prepare Flatbread:
- If using store-bought flatbread, follow the package instructions for pre-baking or heating. If making homemade flatbread, prepare and bake according to the recipe.

Prepare Buffalo Cauliflower:
- Preheat the oven to 425°F (220°C).
- Toss cauliflower florets with olive oil, garlic powder, salt, and black pepper in a bowl.
- Spread the cauliflower on a baking sheet and roast in the preheated oven for 20-25 minutes or until the edges are golden brown and crispy.

Coat Cauliflower in Buffalo Sauce:
- In a separate bowl, mix together buffalo sauce and melted butter.
- Once the cauliflower is done roasting, transfer it to a large mixing bowl and toss it with the buffalo sauce mixture until well coated.

Assemble Buffalo Cauliflower Flatbread:
- If using a pizza stone, transfer the flatbread onto a pizza peel dusted with flour or cornmeal. If not using a stone, place the flatbread on a lightly greased baking sheet.
- Spread an even layer of shredded mozzarella cheese over the flatbread.
- Arrange the buffalo cauliflower evenly on top of the cheese.
- Sprinkle crumbled blue cheese over the cauliflower.
- Bake in the oven for an additional 8-10 minutes or until the cheese is melted and bubbly.

Finish and Serve:
- Remove the flatbread from the oven.
- Sprinkle sliced green onions over the top.
- Drizzle ranch or blue cheese dressing over the flatbread.
- Slice and serve your delicious Buffalo Cauliflower Flatbread!

Enjoy the spicy kick of buffalo sauce paired with the roasted goodness of cauliflower on a crispy flatbread. This recipe is perfect for those looking for a vegetarian twist on a classic buffalo pizza.

Smoked Salmon and Cream Cheese Pizza

Ingredients:

Pizza Dough:

- 2 1/4 teaspoons (1 packet) active dry yeast
- 1 teaspoon sugar
- 3/4 cup warm water (110°F/43°C)
- 2 cups all-purpose flour
- 1 teaspoon salt
- 1 tablespoon olive oil

Pizza Toppings:

- 4 ounces cream cheese, softened
- 1 tablespoon fresh dill, chopped
- 1 tablespoon capers, drained
- 1/2 red onion, thinly sliced
- 4 ounces smoked salmon, thinly sliced
- Fresh lemon wedges for serving
- Freshly ground black pepper

Instructions:

Prepare Pizza Dough:
- In a small bowl, combine warm water, sugar, and active dry yeast. Let it sit for 5-10 minutes until frothy.
- In a large mixing bowl, combine the flour and salt. Make a well in the center and pour in the yeast mixture and olive oil.
- Mix until the dough comes together, then knead on a floured surface for 5-7 minutes or until smooth. Place the dough in an oiled bowl, cover with a damp cloth, and let it rise for 1-2 hours until doubled in size.

Preheat the Oven:
- Preheat your oven to the highest temperature it can go (typically around 475-500°F/245-260°C). If you have a pizza stone, place it in the oven during preheating.

Shape the Pizza Dough:

- Punch down the risen dough and transfer it to a floured surface. Roll it out into your desired pizza shape and thickness.

Assemble Smoked Salmon and Cream Cheese Pizza:
- If using a pizza stone, transfer the rolled-out dough onto a pizza peel dusted with flour or cornmeal. If not using a stone, place the rolled-out dough on a lightly greased baking sheet.
- Spread an even layer of softened cream cheese over the dough, leaving a small border around the edges.
- Sprinkle chopped fresh dill over the cream cheese.
- Scatter capers and thinly sliced red onion over the cream cheese.
- Place slices of smoked salmon evenly on top of the other toppings.

Bake the Pizza:
- If using a pizza stone, carefully transfer the pizza onto the preheated stone in the oven. If not using a stone, simply place the baking sheet in the oven.
- Bake for 10-12 minutes or until the crust is golden, the cream cheese is melted and bubbly, and the edges are slightly crispy.

Finish and Serve:
- Remove the pizza from the oven.
- Squeeze fresh lemon juice over the top.
- Sprinkle freshly ground black pepper.
- Slice and serve your elegant Smoked Salmon and Cream Cheese Pizza!

Enjoy the luxurious combination of smoked salmon and cream cheese on a crispy pizza crust. This pizza is perfect for brunch, lunch, or any occasion where you want to impress with a gourmet twist on a classic favorite.

Sweet Potato and Kale Pizza

Ingredients:

Pizza Dough:

- 2 1/4 teaspoons (1 packet) active dry yeast
- 1 teaspoon sugar
- 3/4 cup warm water (110°F/43°C)
- 2 cups all-purpose flour
- 1 teaspoon salt
- 1 tablespoon olive oil

Pizza Toppings:

- 1 large sweet potato, peeled and thinly sliced
- 2 tablespoons olive oil, divided
- Salt and black pepper to taste
- 2 cups kale, stems removed and chopped
- 2 cloves garlic, minced
- 1 cup shredded mozzarella cheese
- 1/4 cup crumbled feta cheese
- Red pepper flakes (optional, for heat)
- Balsamic glaze (optional, for drizzling)

Instructions:

Prepare Pizza Dough:
- In a small bowl, combine warm water, sugar, and active dry yeast. Let it sit for 5-10 minutes until frothy.
- In a large mixing bowl, combine the flour and salt. Make a well in the center and pour in the yeast mixture and olive oil.
- Mix until the dough comes together, then knead on a floured surface for 5-7 minutes or until smooth. Place the dough in an oiled bowl, cover with a damp cloth, and let it rise for 1-2 hours until doubled in size.

Preheat the Oven:
- Preheat your oven to the highest temperature it can go (typically around 475-500°F/245-260°C). If you have a pizza stone, place it in the oven during preheating.

Roast Sweet Potatoes:
- Toss thinly sliced sweet potatoes with 1 tablespoon of olive oil, salt, and black pepper.
- Spread the sweet potatoes on a baking sheet and roast in the preheated oven for 15-20 minutes or until tender and slightly caramelized. Set aside.

Prepare Kale:
- In a skillet, heat the remaining 1 tablespoon of olive oil over medium heat.
- Add minced garlic and sauté for about 30 seconds until fragrant.
- Add chopped kale and cook until wilted. Season with salt and black pepper. Set aside.

Shape the Pizza Dough:
- Punch down the risen dough and transfer it to a floured surface. Roll it out into your desired pizza shape and thickness.

Assemble Sweet Potato and Kale Pizza:
- If using a pizza stone, transfer the rolled-out dough onto a pizza peel dusted with flour or cornmeal. If not using a stone, place the rolled-out dough on a lightly greased baking sheet.
- Spread an even layer of shredded mozzarella cheese over the dough.
- Arrange the roasted sweet potato slices and sautéed kale evenly on top.
- Sprinkle crumbled feta cheese over the other toppings.
- If desired, add a pinch of red pepper flakes for some heat.

Bake the Pizza:
- If using a pizza stone, carefully transfer the pizza onto the preheated stone in the oven. If not using a stone, simply place the baking sheet in the oven.
- Bake for 10-12 minutes or until the crust is golden, the cheese is melted and bubbly, and the edges are slightly crispy.

Finish and Serve:
- Remove the pizza from the oven.
- Drizzle balsamic glaze over the top if desired.
- Slice and serve your delicious Sweet Potato and Kale Pizza!

Enjoy the combination of sweet and savory flavors along with the nutritional benefits of sweet potatoes and kale in this unique and satisfying pizza. It's a great way to incorporate more veggies into your pizza night!

Provolone and Mushroom Pizza

Ingredients:

Pizza Dough:

- 2 1/4 teaspoons (1 packet) active dry yeast
- 1 teaspoon sugar
- 3/4 cup warm water (110°F/43°C)
- 2 cups all-purpose flour
- 1 teaspoon salt
- 1 tablespoon olive oil

Pizza Toppings:

- 1 1/2 cups sliced mushrooms (such as cremini or button mushrooms)
- 2 tablespoons olive oil
- 2 cloves garlic, minced
- Salt and black pepper to taste
- 1 1/2 cups shredded provolone cheese
- Fresh thyme leaves for garnish (optional)
- Crushed red pepper flakes for optional heat

Instructions:

Prepare Pizza Dough:
- In a small bowl, combine warm water, sugar, and active dry yeast. Let it sit for 5-10 minutes until frothy.
- In a large mixing bowl, combine the flour and salt. Make a well in the center and pour in the yeast mixture and olive oil.
- Mix until the dough comes together, then knead on a floured surface for 5-7 minutes or until smooth. Place the dough in an oiled bowl, cover with a damp cloth, and let it rise for 1-2 hours until doubled in size.

Preheat the Oven:
- Preheat your oven to the highest temperature it can go (typically around 475-500°F/245-260°C). If you have a pizza stone, place it in the oven during preheating.

Prepare Mushroom Toppings:
- In a skillet, heat 2 tablespoons of olive oil over medium heat.

- Add minced garlic and sauté for about 30 seconds until fragrant.
- Add sliced mushrooms to the skillet and cook until they release their moisture and become tender.
- Season with salt and black pepper. Set aside.

Shape the Pizza Dough:
- Punch down the risen dough and transfer it to a floured surface. Roll it out into your desired pizza shape and thickness.

Assemble Provolone and Mushroom Pizza:
- If using a pizza stone, transfer the rolled-out dough onto a pizza peel dusted with flour or cornmeal. If not using a stone, place the rolled-out dough on a lightly greased baking sheet.
- Spread an even layer of shredded provolone cheese over the dough.
- Distribute the sautéed mushrooms evenly on top of the cheese.

Bake the Pizza:
- If using a pizza stone, carefully transfer the pizza onto the preheated stone in the oven. If not using a stone, simply place the baking sheet in the oven.
- Bake for 10-12 minutes or until the crust is golden, the cheese is melted and bubbly, and the edges are slightly crispy.

Finish and Serve:
- Remove the pizza from the oven.
- If desired, sprinkle fresh thyme leaves and crushed red pepper flakes over the top.
- Slice and serve your delicious Provolone and Mushroom Pizza!

Enjoy the robust flavor of provolone cheese combined with the earthy goodness of sautéed mushrooms on a homemade pizza crust. It's a simple yet flavorful pizza that's sure to be a hit!

Artichoke and Sun-Dried Tomato Flatbread

Ingredients:

Flatbread:

- 4 pieces of flatbread (store-bought or homemade)

Artichoke and Sun-Dried Tomato Toppings:

- 1 cup marinated artichoke hearts, drained and chopped
- 1/2 cup sun-dried tomatoes, packed in oil, drained and sliced
- 1/2 cup crumbled feta cheese
- 1/4 cup sliced Kalamata olives
- 2 tablespoons chopped fresh basil
- 2 tablespoons extra-virgin olive oil
- Salt and black pepper to taste

Instructions:

Prepare Flatbread:
- If using store-bought flatbread, follow the package instructions for pre-baking or heating. If making homemade flatbread, prepare and bake according to the recipe.

Assemble Artichoke and Sun-Dried Tomato Flatbread:
- If using a pizza stone, transfer the flatbread onto a pizza peel dusted with flour or cornmeal. If not using a stone, place the flatbread on a lightly greased baking sheet.
- In a bowl, combine the chopped artichoke hearts and sliced sun-dried tomatoes.
- Spread the artichoke and sun-dried tomato mixture evenly over the flatbread.
- Sprinkle crumbled feta cheese and sliced Kalamata olives over the toppings.

Bake the Flatbread:
- If using a pizza stone, carefully transfer the flatbread onto the preheated stone in the oven. If not using a stone, simply place the baking sheet in the oven.

- Bake for 8-10 minutes or until the edges are golden, the cheese is melted, and the toppings are heated through.

Finish and Serve:
- Remove the flatbread from the oven.
- Drizzle extra-virgin olive oil over the top.
- Sprinkle chopped fresh basil.
- Season with salt and black pepper to taste.

Slice and Enjoy:
- Slice the Artichoke and Sun-Dried Tomato Flatbread into portions.
- Serve warm and enjoy your delightful and Mediterranean-inspired flatbread!

This flatbread is perfect for a quick and tasty meal, and it's a great way to savor the delicious combination of artichokes, sun-dried tomatoes, and feta cheese. It's a wonderful option for lunch, dinner, or as an appetizer for gatherings.

Smoky BBQ Bacon Pizza

Ingredients:

Pizza Dough:

- 2 1/4 teaspoons (1 packet) active dry yeast
- 1 teaspoon sugar
- 3/4 cup warm water (110°F/43°C)
- 2 cups all-purpose flour
- 1 teaspoon salt
- 1 tablespoon olive oil

Pizza Toppings:

- 1/2 cup smoky barbecue sauce
- 1 1/2 cups shredded mozzarella cheese
- 1/2 cup cooked and crumbled bacon
- 1/4 cup red onion, thinly sliced
- 1/4 cup fresh cilantro, chopped
- 1/4 cup pickled jalapeños (optional, for heat)
- 1 tablespoon olive oil (for drizzling)

Instructions:

Prepare Pizza Dough:
- In a small bowl, combine warm water, sugar, and active dry yeast. Let it sit for 5-10 minutes until frothy.
- In a large mixing bowl, combine the flour and salt. Make a well in the center and pour in the yeast mixture and olive oil.
- Mix until the dough comes together, then knead on a floured surface for 5-7 minutes or until smooth. Place the dough in an oiled bowl, cover with a damp cloth, and let it rise for 1-2 hours until doubled in size.

Preheat the Oven:
- Preheat your oven to the highest temperature it can go (typically around 475-500°F/245-260°C). If you have a pizza stone, place it in the oven during preheating.

Shape the Pizza Dough:
- Punch down the risen dough and transfer it to a floured surface. Roll it out into your desired pizza shape and thickness.

Assemble Smoky BBQ Bacon Pizza:
- If using a pizza stone, transfer the rolled-out dough onto a pizza peel dusted with flour or cornmeal. If not using a stone, place the rolled-out dough on a lightly greased baking sheet.
- Spread an even layer of smoky barbecue sauce over the dough, leaving a small border around the edges.
- Sprinkle shredded mozzarella cheese over the barbecue sauce.
- Evenly distribute the cooked and crumbled bacon and thinly sliced red onion over the cheese.
- If desired, add pickled jalapeños for a spicy kick.

Bake the Pizza:
- If using a pizza stone, carefully transfer the pizza onto the preheated stone in the oven. If not using a stone, simply place the baking sheet in the oven.
- Bake for 10-12 minutes or until the crust is golden, the cheese is melted and bubbly, and the edges are slightly crispy.

Finish and Serve:
- Remove the pizza from the oven.
- Drizzle olive oil over the top.
- Sprinkle chopped fresh cilantro for a burst of freshness.
- Slice and serve your mouthwatering Smoky BBQ Bacon Pizza!

Enjoy the delightful combination of smoky barbecue sauce and crispy bacon on a homemade pizza crust. This pizza is a crowd-pleaser, perfect for pizza nights and gatherings with friends and family.

Roasted Garlic and Potato Pizza

Ingredients:

Pizza Dough:

- 2 1/4 teaspoons (1 packet) active dry yeast
- 1 teaspoon sugar
- 3/4 cup warm water (110°F/43°C)
- 2 cups all-purpose flour
- 1 teaspoon salt
- 1 tablespoon olive oil

Roasted Garlic Spread:

- 1 head of garlic
- 2 tablespoons olive oil
- Salt and black pepper to taste

Pizza Toppings:

- 1 large potato, peeled and thinly sliced
- 1 tablespoon olive oil
- Salt and black pepper to taste
- 1 1/2 cups shredded mozzarella cheese
- 1/4 cup grated Parmesan cheese
- Fresh rosemary leaves for garnish
- Red pepper flakes (optional, for heat)

Instructions:

Prepare Pizza Dough:
- In a small bowl, combine warm water, sugar, and active dry yeast. Let it sit for 5-10 minutes until frothy.
- In a large mixing bowl, combine the flour and salt. Make a well in the center and pour in the yeast mixture and olive oil.
- Mix until the dough comes together, then knead on a floured surface for 5-7 minutes or until smooth. Place the dough in an oiled bowl, cover with a damp cloth, and let it rise for 1-2 hours until doubled in size.

Preheat the Oven:

- Preheat your oven to the highest temperature it can go (typically around 475-500°F/245-260°C). If you have a pizza stone, place it in the oven during preheating.

Prepare Roasted Garlic Spread:
- Cut the top off the head of garlic to expose the cloves.
- Place the garlic head on a piece of aluminum foil, drizzle with olive oil, and season with salt and black pepper.
- Wrap the garlic in the foil and roast in the preheated oven for 30-40 minutes or until the cloves are soft and golden brown. Allow it to cool.
- Squeeze the roasted garlic cloves out of their skins and mash them into a paste. Set aside.

Prepare Potato Toppings:
- Toss thinly sliced potatoes with olive oil, salt, and black pepper.
- Optionally, you can parboil the potato slices for 2-3 minutes to ensure they cook through during baking.

Shape the Pizza Dough:
- Punch down the risen dough and transfer it to a floured surface. Roll it out into your desired pizza shape and thickness.

Assemble Roasted Garlic and Potato Pizza:
- If using a pizza stone, transfer the rolled-out dough onto a pizza peel dusted with flour or cornmeal. If not using a stone, place the rolled-out dough on a lightly greased baking sheet.
- Spread an even layer of the roasted garlic paste over the dough.
- Sprinkle shredded mozzarella cheese over the garlic spread.
- Arrange the thinly sliced potatoes evenly on top of the cheese.
- Sprinkle grated Parmesan cheese over the potatoes.

Bake the Pizza:
- If using a pizza stone, carefully transfer the pizza onto the preheated stone in the oven. If not using a stone, simply place the baking sheet in the oven.
- Bake for 12-15 minutes or until the crust is golden, the cheese is melted and bubbly, and the edges are slightly crispy.

Finish and Serve:
- Remove the pizza from the oven.
- Sprinkle fresh rosemary leaves over the top.
- Optionally, add red pepper flakes for some heat.
- Slice and serve your delectable Roasted Garlic and Potato Pizza!

Enjoy the comforting combination of roasted garlic and thinly sliced potatoes on a homemade pizza crust. This pizza is perfect for a cozy night in and is sure to satisfy your taste buds with its rich and aromatic flavors.

Bacon, Egg and Cheese Breakfast Pizza

Ingredients:

Pizza Dough:

- 2 1/4 teaspoons (1 packet) active dry yeast
- 1 teaspoon sugar
- 3/4 cup warm water (110°F/43°C)
- 2 cups all-purpose flour
- 1 teaspoon salt
- 1 tablespoon olive oil

Pizza Toppings:

- 1/2 cup pizza sauce or marinara sauce
- 1 1/2 cups shredded mozzarella cheese
- 4 slices of bacon, cooked and crumbled
- 4 large eggs
- Salt and black pepper to taste
- Chopped fresh chives or parsley for garnish (optional)

Instructions:

Prepare Pizza Dough:
- In a small bowl, combine warm water, sugar, and active dry yeast. Let it sit for 5-10 minutes until frothy.
- In a large mixing bowl, combine the flour and salt. Make a well in the center and pour in the yeast mixture and olive oil.
- Mix until the dough comes together, then knead on a floured surface for 5-7 minutes or until smooth. Place the dough in an oiled bowl, cover with a damp cloth, and let it rise for 1-2 hours until doubled in size.

Preheat the Oven:
- Preheat your oven to the highest temperature it can go (typically around 475-500°F/245-260°C). If you have a pizza stone, place it in the oven during preheating.

Shape the Pizza Dough:
- Punch down the risen dough and transfer it to a floured surface. Roll it out into your desired pizza shape and thickness.

Assemble Bacon, Egg, and Cheese Breakfast Pizza:
- If using a pizza stone, transfer the rolled-out dough onto a pizza peel dusted with flour or cornmeal. If not using a stone, place the rolled-out dough on a lightly greased baking sheet.
- Spread an even layer of pizza sauce over the dough, leaving a small border around the edges.
- Sprinkle shredded mozzarella cheese over the sauce.
- Distribute the cooked and crumbled bacon evenly on top of the cheese.

Bake the Pizza:
- If using a pizza stone, carefully transfer the pizza onto the preheated stone in the oven. If not using a stone, simply place the baking sheet in the oven.
- Bake for 8-10 minutes or until the crust is golden, the cheese is melted and bubbly, and the edges are slightly crispy.

Add Eggs:
- Remove the pizza from the oven.
- Crack the eggs onto the pizza, spacing them evenly.
- Season the eggs with salt and black pepper.

Finish Baking:
- Return the pizza to the oven and bake for an additional 5-7 minutes or until the egg whites are set, and the egg yolks are cooked to your liking.

Garnish and Serve:
- Remove the pizza from the oven.
- If desired, sprinkle chopped fresh chives or parsley over the top.
- Slice and serve your delightful Bacon, Egg, and Cheese Breakfast Pizza!

Enjoy the combination of crispy bacon, gooey cheese, and runny eggs on a homemade pizza crust. This breakfast pizza is a crowd-pleaser and a perfect treat for a weekend brunch or any morning when you want a hearty start to the day.

Chicken and Broccoli Alfredo Pizza

Ingredients:

Pizza Dough:

- 2 1/4 teaspoons (1 packet) active dry yeast
- 1 teaspoon sugar
- 3/4 cup warm water (110°F/43°C)
- 2 cups all-purpose flour
- 1 teaspoon salt
- 1 tablespoon olive oil

Alfredo Sauce:

- 1/4 cup unsalted butter
- 2 cloves garlic, minced
- 1 cup heavy cream
- 1 cup grated Parmesan cheese
- Salt and black pepper to taste

Pizza Toppings:

- 1 1/2 cups cooked and shredded chicken breast
- 1 cup broccoli florets, blanched or steamed
- 1 1/2 cups shredded mozzarella cheese
- 2 tablespoons chopped fresh parsley (optional, for garnish)

Instructions:

Prepare Pizza Dough:
- In a small bowl, combine warm water, sugar, and active dry yeast. Let it sit for 5-10 minutes until frothy.
- In a large mixing bowl, combine the flour and salt. Make a well in the center and pour in the yeast mixture and olive oil.
- Mix until the dough comes together, then knead on a floured surface for 5-7 minutes or until smooth. Place the dough in an oiled bowl, cover with a damp cloth, and let it rise for 1-2 hours until doubled in size.

Preheat the Oven:

- Preheat your oven to the highest temperature it can go (typically around 475-500°F/245-260°C). If you have a pizza stone, place it in the oven during preheating.

Prepare Alfredo Sauce:
- In a saucepan over medium heat, melt the butter.
- Add minced garlic and sauté for about 30 seconds until fragrant.
- Pour in the heavy cream and bring it to a simmer.
- Reduce the heat to low and gradually whisk in the grated Parmesan cheese until the sauce is smooth.
- Season with salt and black pepper to taste. Set aside.

Shape the Pizza Dough:
- Punch down the risen dough and transfer it to a floured surface. Roll it out into your desired pizza shape and thickness.

Assemble Chicken and Broccoli Alfredo Pizza:
- If using a pizza stone, transfer the rolled-out dough onto a pizza peel dusted with flour or cornmeal. If not using a stone, place the rolled-out dough on a lightly greased baking sheet.
- Spread an even layer of the prepared Alfredo sauce over the dough.
- Sprinkle shredded mozzarella cheese over the Alfredo sauce.
- Distribute the cooked and shredded chicken and blanched broccoli florets evenly on top of the cheese.

Bake the Pizza:
- If using a pizza stone, carefully transfer the pizza onto the preheated stone in the oven. If not using a stone, simply place the baking sheet in the oven.
- Bake for 10-12 minutes or until the crust is golden, the cheese is melted and bubbly, and the edges are slightly crispy.

Finish and Serve:
- Remove the pizza from the oven.
- If desired, sprinkle chopped fresh parsley over the top.
- Slice and serve your delectable Chicken and Broccoli Alfredo Pizza!

Enjoy the creamy Alfredo goodness paired with the savory chicken and broccoli on a homemade pizza crust. This pizza is a comforting and satisfying choice for a cozy dinner or a special occasion.

Tandoori Chicken Naan Pizza

Ingredients:

Tandoori Chicken:

- 1 pound boneless, skinless chicken thighs or breasts, cut into bite-sized pieces
- 1 cup plain yogurt
- 2 tablespoons tandoori masala
- 1 tablespoon ginger-garlic paste
- 1 tablespoon lemon juice
- 1 teaspoon ground cumin
- 1 teaspoon ground coriander
- 1/2 teaspoon turmeric
- 1/2 teaspoon cayenne pepper (adjust to taste)
- Salt to taste
- 2 tablespoons vegetable oil

Naan Pizza Base:

- 4 pieces of naan bread

Pizza Toppings:

- 1 cup shredded mozzarella cheese
- 1 small red onion, thinly sliced
- 1 small bell pepper, thinly sliced
- Fresh cilantro leaves for garnish
- Lemon wedges for serving

Yogurt Sauce:

- 1/2 cup plain yogurt
- 1 tablespoon chopped fresh mint
- 1 tablespoon chopped fresh cilantro
- Salt and black pepper to taste

Instructions:

    Prepare Tandoori Chicken:

- In a bowl, combine yogurt, tandoori masala, ginger-garlic paste, lemon juice, ground cumin, ground coriander, turmeric, cayenne pepper, salt, and vegetable oil to make the marinade.
- Add the chicken pieces to the marinade, ensuring they are well-coated. Cover and refrigerate for at least 2 hours, or overnight for better flavor.
- Preheat the oven to 400°F (200°C).
- Spread the marinated chicken on a baking sheet and bake for 20-25 minutes or until fully cooked and slightly charred. Set aside.

Prepare Yogurt Sauce:
- In a small bowl, mix together yogurt, chopped fresh mint, chopped fresh cilantro, salt, and black pepper. Set aside.

Assemble Tandoori Chicken Naan Pizza:
- Preheat your oven to the highest temperature it can go (typically around 475-500°F/245-260°C).
- Place naan bread on a baking sheet or pizza stone.
- Spread a generous layer of yogurt sauce over each naan.
- Sprinkle shredded mozzarella cheese evenly over the yogurt sauce.
- Distribute the cooked tandoori chicken pieces on top of the cheese.
- Scatter thinly sliced red onion and bell pepper over the chicken.

Bake the Pizza:
- If using a pizza stone, carefully transfer the naan pizzas onto the preheated stone in the oven. If not using a stone, simply place the baking sheet in the oven.
- Bake for 8-10 minutes or until the cheese is melted and bubbly, and the edges of the naan are golden.

Finish and Serve:
- Remove the pizzas from the oven.
- Garnish with fresh cilantro leaves.
- Serve hot with lemon wedges on the side.

Enjoy the delightful blend of tandoori chicken and traditional pizza elements on naan bread. The cool yogurt sauce complements the spiced chicken, making this Tandoori Chicken Naan Pizza a flavorful and satisfying meal.

Caramelized Onion and Bacon Flatbread

Ingredients:

Flatbread:

- 4 pieces of flatbread (store-bought or homemade)

Caramelized Onions:

- 2 large onions, thinly sliced
- 2 tablespoons unsalted butter
- 1 tablespoon olive oil
- 1 teaspoon sugar
- Salt and black pepper to taste

Flatbread Toppings:

- 1 cup shredded mozzarella cheese
- 1/2 cup crumbled blue cheese or goat cheese (optional, for extra richness)
- 8 slices of cooked bacon, crumbled
- Fresh thyme leaves for garnish (optional)

Instructions:

Prepare Caramelized Onions:
- In a large skillet, heat butter and olive oil over medium-low heat.
- Add thinly sliced onions and cook, stirring occasionally, until they become soft and golden brown, about 20-25 minutes.
- Sprinkle sugar over the onions and continue to cook until they caramelize, becoming sweet and deeply browned.
- Season with salt and black pepper to taste. Set aside.

Prepare Flatbread:
- If using store-bought flatbread, follow the package instructions for pre-baking or heating. If making homemade flatbread, prepare and bake according to the recipe.

Assemble Caramelized Onion and Bacon Flatbread:
- Preheat your oven to the highest temperature it can go (typically around 475-500°F/245-260°C).
- Place flatbread on a baking sheet.

- Spread a layer of caramelized onions evenly over each flatbread.
- Sprinkle shredded mozzarella cheese over the onions.
- If using, crumble blue cheese or goat cheese over the mozzarella.
- Distribute crumbled bacon evenly over the cheeses.

Bake the Flatbread:
- Place the baking sheet in the preheated oven.
- Bake for 8-10 minutes or until the cheese is melted and bubbly, and the edges of the flatbread are golden.

Finish and Serve:
- Remove the flatbread from the oven.
- Garnish with fresh thyme leaves if desired.
- Slice and serve your delicious Caramelized Onion and Bacon Flatbread!

This flatbread is a perfect appetizer or main course, offering a perfect balance of sweet caramelized onions and savory bacon on a crispy crust. It's a great option for entertaining or a cozy night in.

Mediterranean Chicken Pita Pizza

Ingredients:

Pita Pizza Base:

- 4 whole wheat or regular pita bread rounds

Mediterranean Chicken:

- 1 pound boneless, skinless chicken breasts, cut into bite-sized pieces
- 2 tablespoons olive oil
- 1 tablespoon lemon juice
- 2 teaspoons dried oregano
- 1 teaspoon ground cumin
- Salt and black pepper to taste

Toppings:

- 1 cup cherry tomatoes, halved
- 1/2 cucumber, thinly sliced
- 1/4 red onion, thinly sliced
- 1/2 cup crumbled feta cheese
- Kalamata olives, pitted and sliced
- Fresh parsley, chopped, for garnish

Yogurt Sauce:

- 1 cup Greek yogurt
- 1 tablespoon olive oil
- 1 tablespoon lemon juice
- 1 clove garlic, minced
- Salt and black pepper to taste

Instructions:

Preheat the Oven:

- Preheat your oven to 400°F (200°C).

Prepare Mediterranean Chicken:
- In a bowl, combine olive oil, lemon juice, dried oregano, ground cumin, salt, and black pepper to create a marinade.
- Add the chicken pieces to the marinade, ensuring they are well-coated. Allow the chicken to marinate for at least 15 minutes.
- Heat a skillet over medium-high heat. Cook the marinated chicken until fully cooked and slightly browned. Set aside.

Prepare Yogurt Sauce:
- In a small bowl, mix together Greek yogurt, olive oil, lemon juice, minced garlic, salt, and black pepper. Set aside.

Assemble Mediterranean Chicken Pita Pizza:
- Place the pita bread rounds on a baking sheet.
- Spread a generous layer of yogurt sauce over each pita as the base.
- Distribute the cooked Mediterranean chicken evenly among the pitas.
- Arrange cherry tomatoes, cucumber slices, red onion slices, crumbled feta cheese, and Kalamata olives on top of the chicken.

Bake the Pita Pizzas:
- Place the baking sheet in the preheated oven.
- Bake for 8-10 minutes or until the edges of the pita bread are crisp, and the toppings are heated through.

Finish and Serve:
- Remove the pita pizzas from the oven.
- Sprinkle chopped fresh parsley over the top.
- Serve immediately, either whole or sliced into wedges.

Enjoy the delightful combination of tender Mediterranean chicken, crisp veggies, and tangy feta cheese on a pita bread base. This Mediterranean Chicken Pita Pizza is not only delicious but also a quick and easy option for a light meal or appetizer with a Mediterranean twist.

Apple, Bacon and Cheddar Pizza

Ingredients:

Pizza Dough:

- 2 1/4 teaspoons (1 packet) active dry yeast
- 1 teaspoon sugar
- 3/4 cup warm water (110°F/43°C)
- 2 cups all-purpose flour
- 1 teaspoon salt
- 1 tablespoon olive oil

Pizza Toppings:

- 1 cup shredded sharp cheddar cheese
- 1 cup shredded mozzarella cheese
- 6 slices of bacon, cooked and crumbled
- 1-2 medium-sized apples, thinly sliced (use a variety like Granny Smith for a tart flavor)
- 1/4 cup chopped walnuts or pecans
- 2 tablespoons honey
- Fresh thyme leaves for garnish (optional)

Instructions:

Prepare Pizza Dough:
- In a small bowl, combine warm water, sugar, and active dry yeast. Let it sit for 5-10 minutes until frothy.
- In a large mixing bowl, combine the flour and salt. Make a well in the center and pour in the yeast mixture and olive oil.
- Mix until the dough comes together, then knead on a floured surface for 5-7 minutes or until smooth. Place the dough in an oiled bowl, cover with a damp cloth, and let it rise for 1-2 hours until doubled in size.

Preheat the Oven:
- Preheat your oven to the highest temperature it can go (typically around 475-500°F/245-260°C). If you have a pizza stone, place it in the oven during preheating.

Shape the Pizza Dough:

- Punch down the risen dough and transfer it to a floured surface. Roll it out into your desired pizza shape and thickness.

Assemble Apple, Bacon, and Cheddar Pizza:
- If using a pizza stone, transfer the rolled-out dough onto a pizza peel dusted with flour or cornmeal. If not using a stone, place the rolled-out dough on a lightly greased baking sheet.
- Combine shredded sharp cheddar and mozzarella cheese. Spread an even layer of the cheese blend over the pizza dough.
- Distribute the thinly sliced apples, crumbled bacon, and chopped nuts evenly over the cheese.

Bake the Pizza:
- If using a pizza stone, carefully transfer the pizza onto the preheated stone in the oven. If not using a stone, simply place the baking sheet in the oven.
- Bake for 10-12 minutes or until the crust is golden, the cheese is melted and bubbly, and the edges are slightly crispy.

Finish and Serve:
- Remove the pizza from the oven.
- Drizzle honey over the top.
- If desired, sprinkle fresh thyme leaves for a touch of herbaceous flavor.
- Slice and serve your mouthwatering Apple, Bacon, and Cheddar Pizza!

Enjoy the perfect balance of sweet, salty, and smoky flavors in every bite of this unique and delicious pizza. The combination of apples, bacon, and cheddar is a crowd-pleaser and makes for a delightful treat for any occasion.

Buffalo Cauliflower and Blue Cheese Flatbread

Ingredients:

Flatbread Base:

- 4 pieces of flatbread (store-bought or homemade)

Buffalo Cauliflower:

- 1 small head of cauliflower, cut into florets
- 2 tablespoons olive oil
- 1/2 cup buffalo sauce
- 1 tablespoon unsalted butter, melted
- Salt and black pepper to taste

Toppings:

- 1 cup shredded mozzarella cheese
- 1/2 cup crumbled blue cheese
- 2 green onions, thinly sliced
- Fresh cilantro or parsley, chopped, for garnish

Ranch Drizzle:

- 1/2 cup ranch dressing

Instructions:

Preheat the Oven:
- Preheat your oven to 425°F (220°C).

Prepare Buffalo Cauliflower:
- In a large bowl, toss cauliflower florets with olive oil, buffalo sauce, melted butter, salt, and black pepper.
- Spread the coated cauliflower on a baking sheet in a single layer.
- Roast in the preheated oven for 20-25 minutes or until the cauliflower is tender and slightly crispy at the edges.

Prepare Flatbread:

- If using store-bought flatbread, follow the package instructions for pre-baking or heating. If making homemade flatbread, prepare and bake according to the recipe.

Assemble Buffalo Cauliflower and Blue Cheese Flatbread:
- Place the flatbread rounds on a baking sheet.
- Spread a layer of ranch dressing over each flatbread.
- Sprinkle shredded mozzarella cheese over the ranch dressing.
- Distribute the roasted buffalo cauliflower evenly over the cheese.
- Crumble blue cheese on top of the cauliflower.

Bake the Flatbread:
- Place the baking sheet in the preheated oven.
- Bake for 10-12 minutes or until the cheese is melted and bubbly, and the edges of the flatbread are golden.

Finish and Serve:
- Remove the flatbread from the oven.
- Sprinkle thinly sliced green onions and chopped cilantro or parsley over the top.
- Slice and serve your delectable Buffalo Cauliflower and Blue Cheese Flatbread!

Optional: Add Extra Heat:
- For those who love extra heat, drizzle additional buffalo sauce over the flatbread before serving.

Enjoy the spicy, tangy flavor of buffalo cauliflower paired with the creamy goodness of blue cheese on a crispy flatbread. This Buffalo Cauliflower and Blue Cheese Flatbread makes for a delicious and satisfying meal, perfect for game days or as a unique and tasty dinner option.

Shrimp and Avocado Flatbread

Ingredients:

Flatbread Base:

- 4 pieces of flatbread (store-bought or homemade)

Shrimp:

- 1 pound large shrimp, peeled and deveined
- 2 tablespoons olive oil
- 2 cloves garlic, minced
- 1 teaspoon smoked paprika
- Salt and black pepper to taste
- 1 tablespoon fresh lemon juice

Toppings:

- 2 ripe avocados, sliced
- Cherry tomatoes, halved
- Red onion, thinly sliced
- Fresh cilantro or parsley, chopped
- Lime wedges for serving

Creamy Avocado Sauce:

- 2 ripe avocados, peeled and pitted
- 1/4 cup plain Greek yogurt
- 2 tablespoons fresh lime juice
- Salt and black pepper to taste

Instructions:

Preheat the Oven:
- Preheat your oven to 425°F (220°C).

Prepare Shrimp:
- In a bowl, toss shrimp with olive oil, minced garlic, smoked paprika, salt, black pepper, and fresh lemon juice.

- Heat a skillet over medium-high heat. Cook the seasoned shrimp for 2-3 minutes per side or until they are opaque and cooked through.

Prepare Creamy Avocado Sauce:
- In a blender or food processor, combine peeled and pitted avocados, Greek yogurt, fresh lime juice, salt, and black pepper. Blend until smooth and creamy.

Prepare Flatbread:
- If using store-bought flatbread, follow the package instructions for pre-baking or heating. If making homemade flatbread, prepare and bake according to the recipe.

Assemble Shrimp and Avocado Flatbread:
- Place the flatbread rounds on a baking sheet.
- Spread a generous layer of creamy avocado sauce over each flatbread.
- Arrange sliced avocados, cherry tomatoes, and thinly sliced red onion on top of the sauce.
- Distribute the cooked shrimp evenly over the toppings.

Bake the Flatbread:
- Place the baking sheet in the preheated oven.
- Bake for 8-10 minutes or until the flatbread edges are golden and the toppings are heated through.

Finish and Serve:
- Remove the flatbread from the oven.
- Sprinkle chopped cilantro or parsley over the top.
- Serve with lime wedges on the side.

Enjoy the fresh and vibrant flavors of Shrimp and Avocado Flatbread, perfect for a light lunch, dinner, or as an appetizer. The combination of juicy shrimp, creamy avocado, and zesty lime creates a delightful and satisfying dish.

Spinach and Artichoke Dip Pizza

Ingredients:

Pizza Dough:

- 2 1/4 teaspoons (1 packet) active dry yeast
- 1 teaspoon sugar
- 3/4 cup warm water (110°F/43°C)
- 2 cups all-purpose flour
- 1 teaspoon salt
- 1 tablespoon olive oil

Spinach and Artichoke Dip:

- 1 cup fresh spinach, chopped
- 1 cup canned artichoke hearts, drained and chopped
- 1/2 cup mayonnaise
- 1/2 cup sour cream
- 1 cup shredded mozzarella cheese
- 1/2 cup grated Parmesan cheese
- 2 cloves garlic, minced
- Salt and black pepper to taste

Pizza Toppings:

- 1 1/2 cups shredded mozzarella cheese
- Red pepper flakes (optional, for heat)
- Fresh parsley, chopped, for garnish

Instructions:

Prepare Pizza Dough:
- In a small bowl, combine warm water, sugar, and active dry yeast. Let it sit for 5-10 minutes until frothy.
- In a large mixing bowl, combine the flour and salt. Make a well in the center and pour in the yeast mixture and olive oil.
- Mix until the dough comes together, then knead on a floured surface for 5-7 minutes or until smooth. Place the dough in an oiled bowl, cover with a damp cloth, and let it rise for 1-2 hours until doubled in size.

Preheat the Oven:
- Preheat your oven to the highest temperature it can go (typically around 475-500°F/245-260°C). If you have a pizza stone, place it in the oven during preheating.

Prepare Spinach and Artichoke Dip:
- In a bowl, mix together chopped spinach, chopped artichoke hearts, mayonnaise, sour cream, shredded mozzarella cheese, grated Parmesan cheese, minced garlic, salt, and black pepper.

Shape the Pizza Dough:
- Punch down the risen dough and transfer it to a floured surface. Roll it out into your desired pizza shape and thickness.

Assemble Spinach and Artichoke Dip Pizza:
- If using a pizza stone, transfer the rolled-out dough onto a pizza peel dusted with flour or cornmeal. If not using a stone, place the rolled-out dough on a lightly greased baking sheet.
- Spread an even layer of the spinach and artichoke dip over the pizza dough.
- Sprinkle additional shredded mozzarella cheese over the dip.
- If desired, sprinkle red pepper flakes for a bit of heat.

Bake the Pizza:
- If using a pizza stone, carefully transfer the pizza onto the preheated stone in the oven. If not using a stone, simply place the baking sheet in the oven.
- Bake for 10-12 minutes or until the crust is golden, the cheese is melted and bubbly, and the edges are slightly crispy.

Finish and Serve:
- Remove the pizza from the oven.
- Sprinkle chopped fresh parsley over the top.
- Slice and serve your delectable Spinach and Artichoke Dip Pizza!

Enjoy the rich and creamy flavors of spinach and artichoke dip on a pizza crust. This pizza is a fantastic appetizer or main course, perfect for gatherings or a cozy night in.

Pear and Walnut Flatbread

Ingredients:

Flatbread Base:

- 4 pieces of flatbread (store-bought or homemade)

Pear and Walnut Toppings:

- 2 ripe pears, thinly sliced
- 1 cup crumbled goat cheese
- 1/2 cup chopped walnuts
- Honey, for drizzling
- Fresh thyme leaves, for garnish

Instructions:

Preheat the Oven:
- Preheat your oven to 425°F (220°C).

Prepare Flatbread:
- If using store-bought flatbread, follow the package instructions for pre-baking or heating. If making homemade flatbread, prepare and bake according to the recipe.

Assemble Pear and Walnut Flatbread:
- Place the flatbread rounds on a baking sheet.
- Arrange thinly sliced pears evenly over each flatbread.
- Sprinkle crumbled goat cheese and chopped walnuts over the pears.

Bake the Flatbread:
- Place the baking sheet in the preheated oven.
- Bake for 8-10 minutes or until the flatbread edges are golden, and the toppings are heated through.

Finish and Serve:
- Remove the flatbread from the oven.
- Drizzle honey over each flatbread for a touch of sweetness.
- Sprinkle fresh thyme leaves over the top.
- Slice and serve your elegant Pear and Walnut Flatbread!

This flatbread is a perfect appetizer or light meal, showcasing the natural sweetness of pears, the creamy tanginess of goat cheese, and the crunch of chopped walnuts. The addition of honey and fresh thyme adds a beautiful and aromatic touch to the dish. Enjoy the delightful balance of flavors and textures in every bite!

Turkey and Cranberry Pizza

Ingredients:

Pizza Dough:

- 2 1/4 teaspoons (1 packet) active dry yeast
- 1 teaspoon sugar
- 3/4 cup warm water (110°F/43°C)
- 2 cups all-purpose flour
- 1 teaspoon salt
- 1 tablespoon olive oil

Pizza Toppings:

- 1 cup leftover cooked turkey, shredded or sliced
- 1/2 cup cranberry sauce
- 1 1/2 cups shredded mozzarella cheese
- 1/4 cup crumbled feta cheese (optional, for extra richness)
- 1/4 cup chopped pecans or walnuts
- Fresh sage leaves, for garnish
- Salt and black pepper to taste

Instructions:

Prepare Pizza Dough:
- In a small bowl, combine warm water, sugar, and active dry yeast. Let it sit for 5-10 minutes until frothy.
- In a large mixing bowl, combine the flour and salt. Make a well in the center and pour in the yeast mixture and olive oil.
- Mix until the dough comes together, then knead on a floured surface for 5-7 minutes or until smooth. Place the dough in an oiled bowl, cover with a damp cloth, and let it rise for 1-2 hours until doubled in size.

Preheat the Oven:
- Preheat your oven to the highest temperature it can go (typically around 475-500°F/245-260°C). If you have a pizza stone, place it in the oven during preheating.

Shape the Pizza Dough:
- Punch down the risen dough and transfer it to a floured surface. Roll it out into your desired pizza shape and thickness.

Assemble Turkey and Cranberry Pizza:
- If using a pizza stone, transfer the rolled-out dough onto a pizza peel dusted with flour or cornmeal. If not using a stone, place the rolled-out dough on a lightly greased baking sheet.
- Spread a thin layer of cranberry sauce over the pizza dough, leaving a small border around the edges.
- Distribute the leftover cooked turkey evenly over the cranberry sauce.
- Sprinkle shredded mozzarella cheese over the turkey.
- If using, crumble feta cheese over the mozzarella.
- Sprinkle chopped pecans or walnuts over the cheese.
- Season with salt and black pepper to taste.

Bake the Pizza:
- If using a pizza stone, carefully transfer the pizza onto the preheated stone in the oven. If not using a stone, simply place the baking sheet in the oven.
- Bake for 10-12 minutes or until the crust is golden, the cheese is melted and bubbly, and the edges are slightly crispy.

Finish and Serve:
- Remove the pizza from the oven.
- Garnish with fresh sage leaves.
- Slice and serve your delectable Turkey and Cranberry Pizza!

Enjoy the unique and festive flavors of this pizza, making it a perfect way to enjoy holiday leftovers in a creative and delicious manner. The combination of turkey, cranberry, and cheese creates a delightful balance of savory and sweet on a crispy crust.

Fig and Prosciutto Flatbread

Ingredients:

Flatbread Base:

- 4 pieces of flatbread (store-bought or homemade)

Fig and Prosciutto Toppings:

- 1 cup fig jam or preserves
- 8-10 fresh figs, sliced
- 8 slices of prosciutto
- 1 cup crumbled goat cheese
- Balsamic glaze, for drizzling
- Fresh arugula, for garnish
- Salt and black pepper to taste

Instructions:

Preheat the Oven:
- Preheat your oven to 425°F (220°C).

Prepare Flatbread:
- If using store-bought flatbread, follow the package instructions for pre-baking or heating. If making homemade flatbread, prepare and bake according to the recipe.

Assemble Fig and Prosciutto Flatbread:
- Place the flatbread rounds on a baking sheet.
- Spread a generous layer of fig jam or preserves over each flatbread.
- Arrange sliced fresh figs and prosciutto over the fig jam.
- Sprinkle crumbled goat cheese evenly over the toppings.

Bake the Flatbread:
- Place the baking sheet in the preheated oven.
- Bake for 8-10 minutes or until the flatbread edges are golden, and the toppings are heated through.

Finish and Serve:
- Remove the flatbread from the oven.

- Drizzle balsamic glaze over each flatbread for added flavor.
- Scatter fresh arugula over the top.
- Season with a pinch of salt and black pepper to taste.
- Slice and serve your elegant Fig and Prosciutto Flatbread!

This flatbread is perfect as an appetizer for entertaining or as a light and sophisticated meal. The combination of sweet figs, salty prosciutto, creamy goat cheese, and the peppery kick of arugula creates a harmonious and delicious flavor profile. Enjoy the unique and gourmet taste of Fig and Prosciutto Flatbread!

Smoked Gouda and Caramelized Onion Pizza

Ingredients:

Pizza Dough:

- 2 1/4 teaspoons (1 packet) active dry yeast
- 1 teaspoon sugar
- 3/4 cup warm water (110°F/43°C)
- 2 cups all-purpose flour
- 1 teaspoon salt
- 1 tablespoon olive oil

Pizza Toppings:

- 1 cup shredded smoked Gouda cheese
- 2 large onions, thinly sliced
- 2 tablespoons unsalted butter
- 1 tablespoon olive oil
- 1 teaspoon sugar
- Salt and black pepper to taste
- Fresh thyme leaves, for garnish

Instructions:

Prepare Pizza Dough:
- In a small bowl, combine warm water, sugar, and active dry yeast. Let it sit for 5-10 minutes until frothy.
- In a large mixing bowl, combine the flour and salt. Make a well in the center and pour in the yeast mixture and olive oil.
- Mix until the dough comes together, then knead on a floured surface for 5-7 minutes or until smooth. Place the dough in an oiled bowl, cover with a damp cloth, and let it rise for 1-2 hours until doubled in size.

Preheat the Oven:
- Preheat your oven to the highest temperature it can go (typically around 475-500°F/245-260°C). If you have a pizza stone, place it in the oven during preheating.

Caramelize Onions:
- In a large skillet, heat butter and olive oil over medium-low heat.

- Add thinly sliced onions and cook, stirring occasionally, until they become soft and golden brown, about 20-25 minutes.
- Sprinkle sugar over the onions and continue to cook until they caramelize, becoming sweet and deeply browned.
- Season with salt and black pepper to taste.

Shape the Pizza Dough:
- Punch down the risen dough and transfer it to a floured surface. Roll it out into your desired pizza shape and thickness.

Assemble Smoked Gouda and Caramelized Onion Pizza:
- If using a pizza stone, transfer the rolled-out dough onto a pizza peel dusted with flour or cornmeal. If not using a stone, place the rolled-out dough on a lightly greased baking sheet.
- Spread the caramelized onions evenly over the pizza dough.
- Sprinkle shredded smoked Gouda cheese over the caramelized onions.

Bake the Pizza:
- If using a pizza stone, carefully transfer the pizza onto the preheated stone in the oven. If not using a stone, simply place the baking sheet in the oven.
- Bake for 10-12 minutes or until the crust is golden, the cheese is melted and bubbly, and the edges are slightly crispy.

Finish and Serve:
- Remove the pizza from the oven.
- Sprinkle fresh thyme leaves over the top.
- Slice and serve your mouthwatering Smoked Gouda and Caramelized Onion Pizza!

Enjoy the rich and smoky flavor of smoked Gouda paired with the sweetness of caramelized onions on a crispy crust. This pizza is a wonderful choice for a cozy night in or as an impressive appetizer for gatherings.

www.ingramcontent.com/pod-product-compliance
Lightning Source LLC
LaVergne TN
LVHW081551060526
838201LV00054B/1860